By the Same Author

CROWN OF THORNS:
THE DEATH OF THE GREAT BARRIER REEF?
(with Keith Willey)

SHARKS:

The Silent Savages

SHARKS:

The Silent Savages

by Theo W. Brown

A Sports Illustrated Book
Little, Brown and Company
Boston — Toronto

FIFTH PRINTING

Sports Illustrated Books
are published by
Little, Brown and Company
in association with
Sports Illustrated Magazine

LIBRARY OF CONGRESS CATALOGING IN PUBLICATION DATA

Brown, Theo W
  Sharks, the silent savages.

  First published under title: Sharks, the search for a repellent.
  "A Sports illustrated book."
  Includes index.
  1. Sharks—Behavior. 2. Sound-waves—Physiological effect. I. Title.
QL638.B75 1975   597'.31'041825   74-30423
ISBN 0-316-11207-0

PRINTED IN THE UNITED STATES OF AMERICA

For
Kenneth William Murray
and
Dr Louis Malarde

Acknowledgments

Without the support and encouragement of my many friends, including those in the academic world, this book would never have been possible. It would be almost impossible for me to name all those from whom, during so many years, I have received help and advice. To the unnamed, I can only express my deepest gratitude.

I am particularly indebted to my lifelong friend Ronnie Chilcott for her wonderful support, for without this I would have failed long ago; to my brother, Marcus, for his unselfish help with the research undertaking; and to my father for his generous support.

I owe special thanks to Dr Bruce W. Halstead who has fought to keep the project alive, and to his wife, Joy; to Dr Perry W. Gilbert, of the Mote Marine Laboratory, for his continued help and encouragement; and to the Office of Naval Research, United States Navy, and the American Institute of Biological Sciences.

In particular I am indebted to Lieutenant-Colonel Jean Garnier, and Monsieur Andrew Babst for their warm friendship and unfailing assistance, and to Andy's wife, Janene, for her hospitality during my many visits to her home; to the late Dr Louis Malarde, Dr Raymond Bagnis, Dr Saugrain, Monsieur Rolland LeBoucher, and the staff of the Institute of Medical Research of French Polynesia; to Monsieur Claude LeBigot, Monsieur Stien, Jean Tapu and Theodore Cadousteau of the Fisheries Department, and Monsieur Amaru of the Shipping Service in Papeete, Tahiti; and to Dr Yues B. Plessis of the Paris Museum of Natural History.

I am also indebted to the former Governor of the Territory of

French Polynesia, His Excellency Monsieur Sicurani, and to the present Governor, His Excellency Monsieur Pierre Angeli, and to their Administration and the Government of France.

No list of acknowledgments can be complete without mention of my good friends Isobel Bennett and Dr Gordon Grigg of the Zoology Department, University of Sydney, and their continued support and faith in my work; and Professor L. C. Birch, Head of the School of Biological Sciences, University of Sydney, who was good enough to approve my affiliation with his School; and Joe and Laura Fagundes and the boys for their wonderful help.

Lastly I must express my gratitude to my research assistants and student trainees who have tolerated the recent difficult times with never a complaint. These include Stephen McLean and Michael Muchmore, Robert Chilcott and Robert Finch, Tony Ivory, Robert van Prooije and Michael O'Leary.

Foreword

Australians have long been interested in sharks, both as a source of food and as a predator on man. So popular is the school shark —used in "fish-'n'-chips"—that a commercial fishery for this species has recently been threatened because school sharks are now in short supply. Each summer season the Australian Press covers in detail the latest shark attacks on man and recounts past ravages.

In spite of the vivid and chilling accounts of shark attacks, Australians still flock to their beautiful beaches—and for good reason. Australia has the finest system of beach life-guards in the world—and that it is strictly voluntary and well disciplined makes it the more prestigious. In "meshing" Australia also has the most effective method yet devised to protect bathing beaches from sharks. Meshing, introduced first in Australia in 1937, consists simply of fishing for sharks with gill nets and thus reducing the shark population to a point where the ratio of shark to bather is so low that it is highly improbable an attack on a meshed beach will ever occur. In 1957 South Africa followed suit and since that date has also successfully used this method of protecting bathers on its more popular east coast beaches.

But meshing is expensive, for the nets must be tended every other day, dead sharks removed, and nets repaired and reset. Moreover, while meshing protects a beach area, it is of little use to a Scuba diver, to an underwater salvage crew, or to bathers on unmeshed beaches. Other types of shark deterrents are needed, and in recent years research programmes in the United States, sponsored by the Navy's Office of Naval Research and other Federal and private agencies, have yielded a host of anti-shark devices of varying degrees of effectiveness, such as the gas gun, shark screen, infant floatation device, floatation recovery bag, and electric barriers such as the shark shield. All of these devices have their applications and limitations and as yet there is no universal shark deterrent.

One of the most promising recent approaches to the development of a shark deterrent that could have wide applications is the use of sound—both as an attractant and deterrent to sharks. No man has pursued this lead with greater perseverance, imagination, and dedication than has Theo Brown.

In 1964 it was my good fortune to spend a month on Tikehau atoll, French Polynesia, observing the behaviour of sharks in their natural environment and collecting anatomical material for a study of their reproductive system. I was not only impressed by the abundance of sharks and other forms of marine life but also by the clarity of the water which made it possible to photograph in considerable detail the behaviour patterns of the animals we observed. To such an environment, after a distinguished career as a police salvage diver and student of shark behaviour in Australia and New Guinea, came Theo Brown in 1968. Brown set up a small research station on the neighbouring atoll of Rangiroa for the study of sharks and their responses to sonic signals. Under ideal conditions for observation, and with great skill and determination in the face of frequent equipment failures, Theo Brown was able to call in sharks in great numbers with sound signals he had devised. This had been done before by Brown in New Guinea and by Wisby and his colleagues at the University of Miami, Florida, but never with the spectacular success that Brown achieved at Rangiroa. His story of the events that inspired and led him to a study of the role of sounds as both shark attractants and shark deterrents, as told here, is a fascinating one, for Theo Brown is a rare combination of adventurer, diver, conservationist, gifted writer, and above all—a dedicated investigator of shark behaviour.

PERRY W. GILBERT, PH.D.
Director, Mote Marine Laboratory,
Sarasota, Florida and

Professor, Neurobiology and Behaviour,
Cornell University,
Ithaca, New York.

Illustrations

Trainee Robert Chilcott removes young from a shark
Papa and Theodore unload the day's catch
Divers sink the new shark cage into the maelstrom area of the lagoon
Divers at work in the lagoon preparing for experiments
Robert beaches the dinghy in the shallows of the lagoon
Didia and Robert hurry back to the boat
Dolphins swim alongside the author's boat on the Great Barrier Reef
Setting out the shark-catching rig in the lagoon

Between pages 104 and 105

Robert prepares to dive with one of the transducers
Surrounded by a mass of cable, Robert places the transducer on the lagoon floor
The three transducers are set on the edge of the lagoon entrance pass
Dr Bruce Halstead examines a venomous Stone Fish
Dr Don Nelson experiments with underwater sounds on sharks in a tank
Taking blood samples during the dissecting of sharks at Rangiroa
Young sharks ready for birth removed from the mother during dissection
A school of Barracuda attracted by underwater sound transmission
One of the many schools of fish that make Rangiroa Atoll a fisherman's paradise
A deadly sea snake
A huge Manta Ray
Sharks attracted by distress stimulus work themselves into a frenzy
Sharks in a frenzied state fight to reach the source of the attractive signals
Sharks batter themselves to death in the cave concealing the transducer
Student trainee Peter Cox makes the outline of the native rock carvings more distinct with the aid of salt
Watched by native children, divers prepare to dive in the lagoon entrance pass
The author examines a small sea turtle held by Dr Bruce Halstead
Dr Glen Egstrom attaches electrodes to diver Gene Cornelius to record his underwater reactions to sharks
Preparing to dive in the lagoon entrance pass with underwater motion film camera
Student trainee Michael O'Leary peers through the jaws of a large Tiger Shark
Robert swims back to the boat with a shark recovered from set chain lines
Shark specimen killed with an explosive "bang-stick"
Joy Halstead collects marine specimens from the lagoon floor at Rangiroa
Dr Bruce Halstead and assistants gather marine specimens after dark

SHARKS:

The Silent Savages

1

Nothing was further from my mind than sharks as we rowed down Middle Harbour that Saturday afternoon in January of 1960. The air was hot and still, and each dip of the oars sent ripples rushing across the oily-smooth surface of the water towards the shore. The monotonous though pleasant droning of a multitude of cicadas accompanied us as we moved downstream. We had only a short way to row, around the first steep bush-covered point from the boat shed, which was a short distance below the old Roseville traffic bridge. Once we had rounded the point and were opposite the grassy slopes of the Killarney picnic reserve we had reached our destination, a small inlet with a narrow beach of yellow sand. Here the heavy bush timbers grew almost to the water's edge, and the incessant drumming of the cicadas all but drowned our voices. As we lost way and the bow of the dinghy gently rose to meet the slope of the beach, Ken jumped ashore. He was a bright, laughing boy, deeply sun-tanned. Though small for his age of thirteen years, he was an excellent swimmer and a keen underwater enthusiast of both Scuba and skin diving. Ken lived with his parents, Colin and Pauline Murray, his older brother Richard, and his two younger sisters, Glenda and Elizabeth, at Forestville on the far side of Middle Harbour. His companion of the day, Gary Hopkins, was a tall thin lad of sixteen who lived next door to the Murrays.

Gary joined Ken on the beach and they sorted through the flippers, masks and snorkels in preparation for their swim. We had decided to practise skin diving in the harbour to prepare for a dive with underwater breathing equipment at Manly the following day. I had only recently returned to Sydney from Darwin, where I had served with the Northern Territory Police Force. After an absence of almost eleven years, I was staying with my parents in East Lindfield, just across the harbour from Ken's place. I was undecided if I should go to Wellington to take up an appointment in the New Zealand Police Force as a diver on rescue and recovery work, a position I had held in two Australian forces.

The boys entered the water, and I was disappointed when I followed and found it warm and turbid. Even with the aid of my facemask I could see no more than a foot or so under water. As a child I had often swum in these waters and remembered that they had been sparkling and clear. Even at our swimming hole set deep in the surrounding bush a mile or so upstream from the traffic bridge the water had been clear and inviting. Here each summer's afternoon after school we had gathered to splash and play until the fading light sent us hurrying home through the bush. On a sloping rock some of the older boys had fashioned a diving platform of cement down which we rushed before plunging into the water. But that had been over eleven years before, and the waters had long since lost their sparkle, the clearing flow of the tides fighting a losing battle against the flood of waste that had invaded the harbour.

I had met the Murrays on my arrival back in Sydney, the family having recently returned from several years in New Guinea. Ken and I soon found that we had something in common, a love of the marine environment and an urge to explore this fascinating world. And so developed a close friendship that was to end in tragedy— and completely alter my way of life.

The boys splashed and played together for perhaps half an hour, practising duck diving and swimming under water. Gary then left the water, and Ken and I swam several hundred yards out into mid-stream. We swam quietly and slowly together, and I remember on the way back we dived briefly to the harbour floor and, peering through the surrounding gloom, saw the bottom of fine grey sand dotted with an occasional shell. We could see nothing

2

more; the water was too dirty. On reaching the beach, I went ashore, leaving Ken to splash and play about. He started to duck dive in perhaps eighteen feet of water not far from the shore. I turned and spoke to Gary, who was still drying himself with a towel farther up the beach, and as I turned back to Ken I was in time to see him surface with his facemask hanging near his chin. I think I laughed as I called to him, "What's the matter, Ken?' He didn't answer, but just looked at me and gave a soft groan. Again I called, "What's the matter, Ken?" But again he didn't answer, and just kept treading water and looking at me as he gave another soft gasp. I could see something red in the water. "His bathers," I thought; "They're red." But then I saw the red starting to spread through the water under him, and suddenly I knew it was blood. I shall never forget the horror of that moment. I screamed at Gary, "Keep out of the water! Ken's been attacked by a shark." Time ceased to exist. I didn't know I had moved until I was at Ken's side dragging him through the water and then onto the beach. The water was red with blood. Blood was streaming down the wet sand, and it seemed to be everywhere.

I looked up and Gary stood there dumbfounded, staring at us. "The towel, for Christ's sake give me the towel," I screamed. I had to stop the blood; that was all I could think of. Ken's right leg had been torn away above the knee, and the shattered bone was protruding through the remaining flesh. Frantically I wrapped the towel round the wound. My mind was in turmoil. I was crying and praying and I just couldn't think. Ken lay there on the wet sand, fully conscious and just looking at me.

I remembered that I had seen a man and two boys fishing as we rowed round the point, and I told Gary to call for help. Then I could hear the man telling his sons not to get out of their boat, and he helped me lift Ken into the dinghy we had rented from the boatshed. While he rowed I held the towel tightly over Ken's wound and managed to control the bleeding. I fought to control myself, and kept telling Ken that he was going to be all right. I promised him that everything would be O.K. "Does it hurt very much, Ken?" I asked. He replied that it did and closed his eyes. I couldn't stop the tears. I tried to hide my face because I didn't want to upset Ken; but each time I turned he was quietly looking into my eyes, never complaining.

3

I have never felt so helpless, so filled with despair, as during the time it took to reach the boatshed. Dimly I could hear someone calling, "There's been a shark attack, call the ambulance and the police." There was the tinkle of a phone, and then the boatshed owner came running down the landing. I remember he was agitated and he told me, "You shouldn't have been swimming there." I looked at him and he turned away.

We fought our way up the steep track from the boatshed to the main road with Ken on a stretcher. Half-way up we met Pauline, Ken's mother, who had been called to the boatshed by Gary. Gary had followed us in the other row boat with the twelve- and nine-year-old sons of Norman C. Keene, of Ramsay Road, Pennant Hills. It was he who had come to our assistance. He had telephoned Ken's mother, who had rushed to the scene in a neighbour's car.

It was dark when I stood in the corridor with Pauline and Colin Murray as Ken was wheeled from the operating theatre. He was conscious, and as soon as he saw us said, "Can you get me some pyjamas, please, Mum." We stayed with him briefly and then left the hospital, returning the following afternoon. During this visit we talked a little, and I gave him my diver's wrist watch to wear. He was under heavy sedation and dozed fitfully from time to time. As we left Ken was asleep, and I was the last in the room. Before I went through the doorway, I turned, and Ken opened his eyes. We looked at each other for a few seconds without speaking; then he closed his eyes and drifted into sleep again.

Early during the hours of Monday morning Ken's condition suddenly deteriorated and he stopped breathing. For a week the doctors at the hospital fought to save his life. He was placed on an artificial breathing machine, the latest available, which automatically maintained his breathing cycle. It appeared that he had suffered a rare complication that sometimes follows serious bone injury. The fatty substance from the marrow of the bone had entered the blood stream and finally lodged in the fine blood vessels of the brain, causing a collapse of the respiratory system. Ken's heart continued to beat strongly while the doctors fought to dissolve the fatty embolism that was restricting the blood circulation to his brain.

I returned to the hospital on that Monday morning. I couldn't bring myself to leave. Perhaps the doctors and hospital staff knew that I had reached breaking-point, for I was allowed to spend the next seven days in the waiting-room next to Ken's ward, and could visit him as I wished. Pauline and Colin stayed during the first few nights, and then I was alone. They had the rest of their family to look after. Whatever the reason for the tolerance of the hospital staff during that black week I shall never know. I was allowed to use the ward kitchen and Ken's doctors called and saw me on most of their visits.

It was one week later on the following Monday morning that the night nurse came and took me to Ken for the last time. I could see his heart pounding the last desperate beats of life in his veins. He was sinking quickly and I knew that this was the end. I could only stand and look at him. There were no more tears, no more prayers, only the most hopeless feeling that part of myself was dying and that I was completely helpless. Ken died shortly after the arrival of his parents without having regained consciousness.

There followed weeks of unimaginable despair, flooded with periods of such utter loneliness that my very existence seemed pointless. I couldn't forgive myself for what had happened. Why hadn't I thought of sharks? Why Ken and not me? Always the plaguing doubts and questions. But gradually I became able to view the tragedy in its correct perspective. I realized that if it hadn't been for the understanding and compassion of the medical staff of the Royal North Shore Hospital during that first terrible week I could never have borne the loss I suffered. Somehow being able to stay with Ken to the very last gave me the strength and the mental crutch I needed to steer me through the period that followed. I felt I owed a deep debt of gratitude, and became convinced that there had to be a reason, that all things must have a purpose no matter how obscure this may be.

I would lie awake deep into the night turning over the facts of the incident, and trying to find the answers to the questions that presented themselves. Why had the attack taken place? Why had there been no attacks when I was a boy, swimming regularly in the same area each summer? What could be done to stop other such tragedies? I knew it would be pointless telling people, particularly children, that it was unsafe to swim in the harbour, or anywhere else for that matter. A hot day and cool, inviting water presented an irresistible attraction to most, enough to fade even the most vivid memories of danger. Without realizing when, I suddenly knew that I could find a purpose in Ken's tragic death if others could be protected from the horror of shark attack. And so started a quest that was to lead me half-way round the world in the search for the elusive, all-purpose shark repellent.

Before I could hope to go any further with my plans, I knew I must learn all I could about sharks. So I began a detailed study of all the available literature, spending long hours at the public libraries checking and rechecking all known information on shark repellents, on the behaviour pattern of sharks, and on their general biology. I approached the leading Australian shark expert, the late Dr Victor Coppleson, who was later to be knighted for his services to the community, as well as other senior world authorities on the subject, and so got further valuable assistance in my search for knowledge. It soon became alarmingly evident how little was really known about sharks: not one of the known shark repellents or deterrents being employed to protect man from the dangers of shark attack could be classed as even moderately successful or reliable.

The first concentrated effort to obtain a satisfactory shark repellent was made by the United States Navy during World War II. In 1942 scientists from the Office of Naval Research in Washington, under the leadership of Stewart Springer, formed a team to look for a shark repellent. Poisoned meat didn't work. Even baits injected with the strongest poisons known proved useless, for the flesh was taken and consumed. It was immaterial that the sharks died half an hour later: the point was that they had swallowed the bait. Various types of ink clouds also failed, for sharks were found to use their sense of smell more than their sight. Even so, when a variety of war and industrial gases, stenches and irritants were experimented with these also proved useless. Then Stewart Springer tried decomposing shark meat, and this worked. Rotten shark flesh four to six days' old proved very distasteful to the sharks. By distilling the rotten flesh it was found that the "x" factor working as a repellent was ammonium acetate; and further experimental work revealed that the exact agent was acetic acid, given off when ammonium acetate is dissolved in water. It was then discovered by Dr A. McBride that copper sulphate was an even more effective repellent than the extract from decomposing shark meat. The research team eliminated numerous other agents and finally chose copper acetate, a double-barrelled repellent composed of Springer's acetic acid and McBride's copper sulphate.

In tests off the South American coast at Posorja the copper acetate proved successful in keeping sharks away from set baits. It was argued by other scientists that when large numbers of sharks were present the olfactory sense ceased to play a dominant part in directing a shark to its prey, and when there was a mob frenzy the sharks attacked on their visual and auditory senses. If it was correct that sharks "switched off" their sense of smell in a feeding frenzy, how could a chemical repellent work under those conditions? The Navy then decided to produce a mixture of one part copper acetate to four parts of negrosine-type dye, the dye being employed to hide the swimmer from the sharks' view, just as the octopus exudes a dye for defence. The repellent was manufactured into solid cakes with a water-soluble wax, enabling it to dissolve rapidly on contact with salt water. It was issued to the armed services and became known as "Shark Chaser".

I decided to conduct my own evaluation programme on "Shark Chaser" and obtained a number of large plastic bags filled with a powdered form of the repellent. After my decision to experiment in the field of shark repellents, I had established myself in 1961 on Magnetic Island, pleasantly situated about five miles from Townsville in Cleveland Bay. Here in North Queensland and close to the Great Barrier Reef there was an abundance of sharks, and conditions would be ideal in the tropical climate for the research work I planned. It was from the island that the first tests were made on possible forms of shark repellents.

The local waters abounded in large sharks of a number of species, and many were taken on set lines for specimen study, and to gain the necessary first-hand experience by dissecting and learning the biology of sharks. The local island policeman, Jack Frame, who was a keen fisherman, enthusiastically engaged in the shark-catching programme, and caught many excellent specimens for me with his specially designed drum catching equipment. He was forced to give up helping me because some of the local people objected, complaining that our activities were damaging the tourist potential of the island. Since most of the residents derived their livelihood from the tourist industry, and since I realized that sharks and tourists didn't go together, I decided to conduct all further experimental work in secret. Many of the beautiful and picturesque bays dotted around the island were uninhabited and surrounded by lush bushland that supported a variety of wildlife: brilliantly coloured and exotic birds, downy-soft koala bears, possums and wallabies. In these localities I could work with sharks quietly and carefully. Apart from the experimental work I was conducting whenever possible, I had to find suitable employment to supply the means to support the programme. Finding that outside work was too restricting and demanding in terms of time, I hit upon the idea of establishing a tourist boat service. With financial assistance from my father in Sydney, I bought a high-speed launch and arranged round-island cruises and fast trips to and from Townsville to augment the regular ferry service operated by Hayle's Magnetic. I was thus able to devote the majority of my time to my consuming passion—shark research.

To evaluate the U.S. Navy's "Shark Chaser", I chose Coil Reef, a small patch of coral situated about seventy miles north-east of Townsville on the extreme outer edge of the Great Barrier Reef. Here, where the corals are exposed to the full fury of the Pacific swells, and where the reef is exposed only at very low tide, there was an abundance of large, dangerous sharks. It was a perfect day with nothing more than a gentle swell, the oily-smooth surface of the water reflecting the burning tropical sun. On looking down through the crystal clear water on the open ocean side of the reef, I could make out the faint outline of the coral reef edge tumbling downwards perhaps a hundred or so feet before it disappeared into the deep blue void of the Pacific. The area was well known to local fishermen for its hungry and vicious sharks, and I felt a tinge of excitement as I prepared the first 44-gallon drum full of blood and offal and emptied its contents into the water. A number of such drums had been obtained from the local Townsville meatworks, and had been brought here in a chartered fishing-boat. The water around the boat was soon crimson in every direction, contrasting vividly with the deep indigo blue of the ocean.

Before the last of the drums had been discharged into the sea the first sharks appeared, smaller than I had anticipated, their presence betrayed by their slowly moving dorsal fins as these cut a wake through the now foaming red water. Soon other larger sharks arrived, at first cautiously circling the outer limits of the blood, then charging headlong into the stained area that completely surrounded the boat. I watched fascinated as the sharks circled closer to the side of the boat and the large baits that had been secured there. The dancing fins were no longer gracefully gliding through the water; their effortless movement had become agitated and violent as the sharks sliced viciously from side to side.

Suddenly a large shark thudded against the side of the boat as it seized half a side of beef set as bait. In its frantic efforts to tear the flesh apart it lifted its giant head from the water, its eyes rolled back, white and staring. I quickly tore open one of the plastic bags of "Shark Chaser" and spilled the contents into the sea and over the shark. Its violent thrashing as it sought to tear the bait apart turned the water from red to black as the repellent quickly spread. But it seemed to have little effect, and hurriedly I shouted to the crew to open and scatter the contents of further bags, for the boat was now virtually surrounded by sharks, rushing and snapping at the offered baits, thrashing through the dye-blackened sea. Still more of the repellent was cast into the water with little effect.

The sharks were becoming too numerous to count. Suddenly the sea seemed to boil as the sharks exploded into a frenzy of activity. In desperation I flung an unopened bag of repellent into the midst of a pack of sharks fighting to tear the remaining baits apart. To my astonishment it was instantly devoured. Hurriedly I threw the remaining bags into the mêlée and these too were consumed. By this time a gleeful crew had commenced to pelt the sharks with pieces of wood, empty bottles and beer cans, pieces of metal, in fact anything not of value that was movable. All were greedily devoured as they struck the water. The surrounding sea was foaming red and black as the sharks suddenly turned upon themselves and began to tear one another apart in a sickening orgy. Nothing escaped untouched. Even the boat shuddered from time to time as sharks fruitlessly sought to smash through its stout timbers, small flakes of paint appearing on the surface to mark their frantic efforts.

Several empty 4-gallon drums were thrown overboard and these too disappeared with sickening crunches as the frenzied feeding of the sharks continued. I heard a shout, and was in time to see an empty 44-gallon drum splash into the water. In an instant it was surrounded by sharks and, unbelievably, it was dragged beneath the surface, to pop up again and then vanish completely without a trace. I was stunned. I had witnessed an unparalleled orgy of uncontrolled fury, a fascinating and repulsive display of strength beyond belief, of primitive animal against primitive animal.

Then suddenly the sharks were gone. The foaming and splashing ceased and the waters resumed their deceptive oily appearance, vividly coloured with splashes of black and crimson that were the only remaining evidence of the holocaust. The once gleeful crew of hardened fishermen stood quietly on deck, surveying the coloured waters and remembering the awesome scene. It had been as though we had been cast back into the primitive beginnings of the earth by such a spectacle, so divorced from our way of life, so different from our knowledge of living things.

And I was shocked beyond the shock of this experience: for now I knew that no chemical repellent could hope to work under such conditions, nor could anything that depended on the visual apparatus of sharks. I became plagued with doubts. Could anything hope to work when such a thing occurred? It was obvious that an entirely new approach would be necessary if success was to be achieved.

I could now eliminate chemical repellents that acted on the sense of smell, as well as coloured dyes or other materials that acted on the visual apparatus of sharks. Even if successful, a chemical repellent would be too subject to water movements and currents, and would disperse fairly rapidly. And any repellent that depended on the sharks' visual apparatus would be useless in turbid or discoloured water where underwater visibility was minimal. This would eliminate its successful application in harbour and surf-beach areas, where turbid water conditions are usual, and at the site of a disaster at sea, which is always associated with discoloured water.

However, the wartime value of "Shark Chaser" could not be dismissed. Although research had yielded such conflicting results, the repellent had at least some psychological value to the user at a time that this was needed most.

I next turned my attention to the so called "Bubble Barrier" repellent, invented by Frank Arpin of Western Australia. This consisted of a plastic garden hose punctured with a series of holes through which compressed air was forced by means of a compressor. When it was laid along the sea floor, the resulting bubble curtain was said to repel sharks effectively (as reported in the Perth *Daily News* on 28th October 1960): "The sharks are so terrified by the shark fence that they will not cross it even to get a juicy steak, according to the inventor. . . ." So impressed was the general public with the "Bubble Barrier", both in Australia and overseas, that at Sea Girt, New Jersey (U.S.A.), a perforated hose 350 feet long was placed on the sea floor between two jetties, 200 feet off shore from a popular bathing beach and, according to a local hotel manager, the bubble fence proved to be "absolutely impenetrable" to sharks.

Following considerable publicity about the merits of the "Bubble Barrier" and optimistic statements about its effectiveness in keeping large and dangerous sharks at bay, a detailed investigation was undertaken by Dr Perry W. Gilbert, of Cornell University. Dr Gilbert, regarded by many as the foremost authority in the world today on shark repellents and the behaviour pattern of sharks, conducted a series of experiments during March and April of 1961. The tests were conducted at the Lerner Marine Laboratory at Bimini in the Bahamas. The tests showed conclusively that many of the sharks used in the experiments soon adjusted to the presence of the "Bubble Barrier" and would pass freely through the air curtain completely unperturbed.

Although electrical barriers have been partially successful during experimental work in stopping and repelling sharks, important difficulties in the complexity of design and in cost need to be overcome before these can be practical. And even if electrical barriers could be perfected their application would be limited to protecting bathing areas, such as beaches. A recently invented electronic shark repeller has obvious disadvantages. When a trigger is pulled, an electrified zone is set up adjacent to the end of a wand. The operator is six feet from the electrified zone at the end of the wand and doesn't get shocked. Sharks are said to retreat when they come into contact with the electrical field. But it is necessary for the operator to carry the six-foot pole or wand, to which is attached the repelling device, and the shark moves dangerously close before the repellent is effective. I decided that these electrical methods did not warrant further evaluation: they did not meet the requirements of an all-purpose repellent.

Dr C. Scott Johnson's "Shark Survival Sack", although it proved successful under certain test conditions, had the disadvantage of being extremely limited in its use. Designed in the United States, this device consists of a plastic container supported by several inflatable rings into which the survivor of a tragedy at sea places himself. Although the plastic container has proved to be successful under some conditions, having isolated the person in the water from the sensory systems of cruising sharks, its usefulness to the survivors of a major tragedy at sea would be extremely limited. The disorder and panic that usually follow such an occurrence would allow little time for the survivors to be equipped with this form of shark protection.

A continuing programme to evaluate possible shark repellents is being conducted by the Mote Marine Laboratory under Dr Perry Gilbert. A deterrent initially developed by Dr H. D. Baldridge at the Mote Laboratory, and now used by the U.S. Navy, is the gas gun. Navy frogmen used the device on the Apollo 15 and 16 splashdowns when inflating the buoyancy collar around the capsule. High-pressure gas is injected into the body of a shark by means of a projectile fired from a gun. This rapidly inflates the body cavity of the shark with gas, making the animal incapable of further underwater movement. But again this method is greatly restricted in its possible application.

In evaluating shark repellents or deterrents, the basic aim must always be to protect the survivors of a disaster at sea. The protection of swimmers in coastal regions is secondary. Although a number of humans are attacked and fatally mauled each year along our beaches and in harbours, tidal creeks, rivers and estuaries, it is at sea that the greatest danger from shark attack is ever-present.

The history of shark repellents has proved to be one of continued failure, and this I find amazing when we consider that man, who has conquered space, cannot as yet adequately protect himself from one of the most primitive forms of life on this planet.

Perhaps meshing is the only measure that has provided a reasonable safeguard from the dangers of shark attack. Shark meshing was introduced on the east coast of Australia in 1937, and it has been in use ever since, apart from a break of several years during World War II. Anchored gill nets are placed near to a bathing or surf beach, and the gill nets catch sharks as they approach the beach area or leave it. The Australian record of success for meshing is impressive, with only two attacks having occurred in a meshed area since its introduction. In 1952 the authorities of Durban, South Africa, also began meshing, with several nets, each 450 feet long, placed parallel to the beach at about 1,500 feet off shore. These had an equal record of success. It would appear that meshing owes its remarkable success to the fact that many sharks, excluding the pelagic or open ocean species, establish themselves in a "house" or "domicile area", or alternatively have a set region that they patrol systematically. Meshing effectively wards off or eliminates the sharks that frequent the waters adjacent to the bathing or surf beach, and so the threat of shark attack is greatly reduced. The decline in the numbers of sharks taken each year in any given area, since the introduction of meshing, tends to support this theory.

Unfortunately, meshing activities also result in the elimination of many harmless fish and other marine animals that happen to blunder into the gill nets and perish. It is important to realize, too, that the continued reduction of the large predators in any locality can have serious long-term effects on the ecology of the region. Instead of improving the fishing potential, meshing in some areas has resulted in a marked reduction in the bony fish population. Whether this is directly related to meshing activities remains to be proved.

Shark meshing cannot be considered foolproof, for the danger of shark attack always remains, even in regions so protected. The method can be employed only to safeguard open swimming and surf beaches where the placing of nets will not interfere with shipping. It cannot be used for harbours, tidal rivers, creeks and estuaries, where many of our coastal shark attacks occur. And shark meshing cannot be used to protect the survivors of a tragedy at sea. But there is ample evidence that its introduction has greatly reduced the threat of shark attack along some of the world's most popular surfing and swimming beaches. Until some practical alternative is perfected, the disadvantages of meshing are far outweighed by the record of its success.

The more I investigated the many failures recorded for shark repellents, the more involved and impossible the task I had set myself seemed to become. Any shark repellent to be completely effective must be capable of deterring all species of known or reputed man-eating sharks under all circumstances. The repellent must be effective immediately; and once in the water it must have long-lasting potency at an effective strength. Since aviation and marine accident survivors often drift for days before being rescued, the repellent must last for seventy-two hours or more. It must be automatically actuated by contact with water in order to protect wounded, disabled or temporarily unconscious people. In addition, the repellent must be self-operating, and must be designed so that it can operate continuously and also be used intermittently when required. It must be effective over a wide area and to a reasonable depth; and finally, the repellent package must be small and light, safe and convenient, and relatively inexpensive.

I started to doubt my capacity to achieve success in a field where so many others had failed. Would I ever be able to solve the long list of problems that had to be solved before my goal could be reached, to find a repellent that could fulfil so many roles? A despondent letter to my brother, Marcus, brought a reply that ended: "It is better to have tried and failed than not to have tried at all."

I determined to push on to the bitter end: and then suddenly I realized that perhaps I already held the key to success.

2

Since the dawn of history, man, through his first primitive drawings and written documents, has made known his fear of sharks. As a boy in Sydney, while bush walking with my father in the then untouched bushlands surrounding our home at East Lindfield, I came across what could have been the first recorded evidence of a shark attack in Australian waters. Set deep in the bush above Middle Harbour, close to where the Wakehurst Parkway is now situated, we located a huge expanse of flat rock dotted with Aboriginal carvings. One of these outlines in the rock graphically illustrated a huge shark, with mouth agape, about to seize a girl or woman. Already this pathetic-looking figure bore the marks of attack, the native artist having drawn deep and jagged gashes on the body to represent tooth marks. Who knows what tales of horror unfolded on the silent harbour waters, and how many natives were dragged to their death by sharks?

Man has sought in vain to devise some method of protecting himself against the dangers of shark attack. What tragedies there must have been at sea over the ages, and what tragedies there still are! Consider this account of the torpedoing of a British cruiser in the South Atlantic on 7th December 1941:

> As the burning cruiser settled in the water, injured and bleeding men jumped over the side and splashed towards life

15

rafts. Blood from open wounds began to diffuse around the swimmers. Panicky, jerky splashing movements from wounded men echoed outwards through the water.

The first sharks to arrive immediately attacked the struggling swimmers. Razor teeth sheared into screaming men and sliced away large mouthfuls of flesh. Limbs were chopped off in single bites; severed arteries pumped yet more blood into the water. The ocean foamed red as more sharks arrived and feasted on the helpless survivors.

There is little a man can do to defend himself once a shark attack is launched. The lucky ones clawed their way aboard the rafts and beat at the snapping sharks with paddles and flotsam. The screams of the injured and dying mingled with the curses of the living, and then there was silence.

When the shocking feast was over, 280 men had died. Only 170 of the cruiser's complement of 450 men survived the torpedoing and frenzy feeding of the sharks.

No one knows how many seamen and fliers were devoured by sharks during World War II. Not even the toll taken in our coastal regions can be accurately assessed: many of the people supposed drowned, with no subsequent recovery of the body, may have been shark-attack victims. And many of the horrors that have occurred at sea have been either deliberately unrecorded by the authorities or unwitnessed except by the all-embracing sea.

The impact of an aircraft striking the water, the noises of a dying ship, the exploding boilers and grinding plates: these bring all the sharks in the vicinity hurrying to the scene. And when there is a tragedy at sea, we invariably have injured survivors. Here, then, are the ingredients for a shark feeding orgy. A few grim reports of these occurrences have filtered through to the general public. When the troop ship *Nova Scotia* was lost off the South African coast in November of 1942, it was recorded that perhaps a thousand men fell victim to the frenzied feeding of the pack of sharks that soon arrived at the disaster site. More recently, in November of 1967, a ferry boat carrying over thirty children sank off the coast near Manila in the Philippines. Many of the survivors were attacked and killed by sharks, and those rescued told of how the sea turned red with blood. During 1969 a DC-9 airliner was forced to ditch in the Caribbean. It was evident from the body remains recovered, most of which were equipped with fully in-flated life jackets, that most if not all the passengers and crew had survived the impact and ditching of the aircraft into the sea. But they had all perished from being shockingly mauled and mutilated by sharks.

Although there are between 250 and 300 species of sharks found throughout the ocean systems and waterways of the world, only a few of these are considered dangerous to man. The known or reputed man-eating sharks number only about twelve species. Sharks are among the few remaining creatures that have passed through the aeons practically unchanged by evolution. They have been in existence for well over 300 million years and need no improvement. Because they are so efficient, they have remained relatively unaltered for almost 200 million years, so perfectly have they adapted themselves to the changing environment. Graceful, streamlined, and deadly efficient, they are the killers of the old and the weak, being perhaps the most powerful living creatures on this planet today. It is said that sharks were the first living animals to develop teeth, and physiologists have told us that all other animals, both marine and terrestrial, including man, have followed the lead given by sharks.

The Elasmobranchs or strap-gilled fishes, as the sharks and rays are called, have the sub-class of Elasmobranchii, further divided into two orders, of which Squaliformes includes the various families of sharks. They are among the lowest and most primitive group of backboned animals and are found in most waters of the world, including fresh water. Sharks range in size from a few inches at maturity to giants like the Whale or Checkerboard Shark, which can be between 70 and 75 feet in length. They occur in depths ranging from the shallowest water to thousands of feet in the great oceans, being most abundant in tropical and semi-tropical areas. Sharks are still numerous in the temperate regions and several species are known to inhabit the waters of the Arctic and Antarctic.

All sharks are essentially carnivorous and predatory, and their diet ranges from man himself down to crustaceans, sea urchins, and in some cases to the lowly sea worms. In both their living and extinct form sharks are remarkable in that they have no bony skeleton as do the higher fishes or Teleostomes (bony fish). The skeleton is wholly cartilaginous or partly calcified, that is, hardened by the addition of calcareous or limey matter. The skin may be smooth, or extremely rough, being covered with minute denticles, which when examined closely are remarkably similar to the teeth of the shark. The skin of many sharks is capable of inflicting serious or fatal injuries through its abrasive contact, and a number of human fatalities have occurred from the bumping or "feeling" activities of sharks when they have approached their victims in this manner. Likewise the fins, particularly the large pectoral fins on each side, as well as the dorsal fins on the top of the body and the tail or caudal fins, are capable of inflicting shocking injury if contact is made with a rapidly moving shark.

I remember during 1958, while diving at the Cocos-Keeling Islands, I had good cause to become aware of the destructive power of a shark's fins. Situated about half-way between Perth and Colombo, in the Indian Ocean, the Cocos Islands consist of a circle of twenty-seven coconut- and jungle-covered coral islets that emerge from the rim of an extinct volcano. North Keeling Island is situated fifteen miles due north of the main group, and became well known to many after the sinking of the German raider *Emden* during the First World War by the Australian Navy warship *Sydney*. The remains of the wreck, including the boilers, are still visible on the coral-covered reefs close off the shore of the island.

The waters of the lagoon at Cocos, particularly in the main entrance pass, were the clearest I have encountered anywhere in the world, and so was the open ocean beyond the pass. My first dive was in the entrance pass, at a point where the lagoon floor dropped from a gradual coral-covered slope, at between a hundred and a hundred and fifty feet, to form a sheer cliff plunging thousands of feet into the unknown. I found the water was unnaturally clear as, with my diving equipment, I jumped into the water. Seconds later I was frantically clawing at the side of the boat for fear I would crash onto the reef about 120 feet below. The sea appeared sterile; there was no suspension of any kind; just nothing —apart from the fish that appeared to be flying and floating far below; and for one terrible moment I had visions of falling onto the rocks. It was so clear that I found the scene unnerving, and it took me several dives before I adjusted to these new surroundings.

18

It was while returning from a dive in the lagoon that I had my chance encounter with a shark and learnt of its bumping tactics. I had swum several hundred yards out from Direction Island alone, in order to record the colourful marine life on a coral "bombie" that rose suddenly from the pure white sand of the lagoon floor. Although sharks were numerous in the lagoon and surrounding waters, I paid little attention to them. They were, for the most part, timid and kept well clear of divers. I was carrying my camera, in a heavy metal underwater housing, loosely in my hands as I swam along the surface, idly watching the underwater landscape glide past. Suddenly I experienced a violent jolt and the camera case was wrenched from my grasp and sent spinning to the lagoon floor. At the same time a large shark swept inches beneath me and, without pausing, disappeared into the surrounding gloom. I was badly shaken and dived down to recover my camera equipment before hurriedly swimming for the shore. Later on when ruefully examining the camera case, I found that it had been completely stripped of several layers of paint and, where the gleaming metal had been exposed, was bent inwards from the impact of the shark's dorsal fin. I was fortunate indeed that it was the underwater housing that had taken this impact.

During my stay of seven months on the tiny atoll that is owned by one John Clunies-Ross by virtue of a royal proclamation from the British Crown to his ancestors, there were two cyclones that swept close. Considerable damage was caused by the second of these, which sent huge seas cascading across some of the islands whose maximum elevation is only seven feet above sea level. Normally, the surrounding coral reefs offer ample protection and keep the ocean at bay. Portions of the international airstrip on West Island were swept away, and the Department of Civil Aviation air-sea rescue base on Direction Island suffered extensive damage to its marine craft. I was to assist in the salvage of several of these in the days that followed and, while working on a large landing barge that had sunk, I received the continual attention of a small white-tip reef shark. The job took several days of diving activity, and each morning as soon as I entered the water the shark was waiting near the wreck, never aggressive, perhaps just curious.

So abrupt was the cliff-like decline of the atoll sides that water several thousands of feet deep was to be found only a few yards from the palm-covered shores. Fascinated by this underwater world, I spent many hours recording the marine life on the various levels of this steep drop-off, exploring down to the extreme limit of my diving equipment, which was around 200 feet. At this depth I could peer directly down into the void beneath me, and occasionally I would glimpse the shadowy form of some large shark or other marine creature as it moved for a moment within the limits of the sunlight.

So deep was the water close to the atoll, that the P. & O. liners of the day often swept close to the islands, so close that, looking out of my quarters on Direction Island, I could see the hundreds of passengers lining the rails peering down on me from the towering sides of the liner as they were rushed past in a blur of faces.

Most sharks give birth to living young, although a few of the smaller species produce and deposit eggs. The number of living young born at the one time varies considerably with each species of shark, and perhaps the Tiger Shark is one of the most prolific breeders, being known to give birth to fifty-seven offspring in the one batch. The newborn sharks must fend for themselves, and it is not uncommon for them to be consumed by their own mother. One species of shark is a cannibal even before it is born. The eggs of the Sand Tiger hatch within the uterus, where the young remain until they have sufficiently developed to enter the ocean. The first baby hatched feeds on its weaker brothers and sisters as they emerge from other eggs. As there are two separate uteruses, two young Sand Tigers survive to be born. This is the only known intra-uterine cannibalism in the animal world and was discovered by Stewart Springer while he was examining a pregnant shark and was bitten on the hand by an unborn baby!

The teeth of sharks are not planted in sockets, but are simply embedded in the "gums" and connected to the jaws by a kind of fibrous tissue. As in nearly all fishes, sharks have their teeth renewed as fast as the old ones are worn out or are dislodged. In most sharks the teeth are arranged in a number of rows, sometimes twenty-eight or so in number. Only the first row (the functional teeth) is erect; the other rows of teeth, which are in various stages of development, lie back inwards, and are hidden beneath a protecting fold of membrane.

Among the sharks the greatest diversity of form is to be found in the teeth. These range from the tiniest prickles or knobs, in some of the small sharks, to the great triangular fangs of the White Shark. There are the comb-like teeth of the One-finned Sharks, the long, owl-like fangs of the Grey Nurse, the larger pointed fangs of the Blue Pointer, the crosscut-saw teeth of the Tiger Shark, the spine-like thorns in the mouth of the Frilled Shark, and a host of other shapes and sizes.

No other fish can match a shark in jaw power. Dr Perry Gilbert has measured this force with an ingenious apparatus he helped to perfect. The bite of a shark is measured in tons, not pounds. After experimental work at the Lerner Marine Laboratory, Dr Gilbert employed the "bite meter" designed by James Snodgrass of the Scripps Institute of Oceanography. Basically the bite meter consists of a cylinder ten inches or so in length containing an aluminium core of known hardness enclosed by four quadrants of steel. Twelve stainless-steel bearings lie between the two layers. Bait is wrapped around the device to attract sharks, which soon clamp down hard on the apparent meal. Knowing the force required to dent the aluminium core, Dr Gilbert was able to estimate that an 8½-foot Dusky Shark had a biting pressure of approximately eighteen tons to the square inch!

Unlike the bony fish, which have a gas-filled bladder that can be adjusted to allow the fish to "float" at various depths under water, sharks have none. Once a shark ceases to move it sinks, and it is not unusual to see the coastal species resting on the sea floor in comparatively shallow water. But the pelagic sharks that frequent the deep oceans must continue moving from the moment of birth to the moment of death, for to stop swimming would send them sinking down into the crushing pressures deep below.

During the many years I have been dissecting sharks, and examining and recording the stomach contents, I have come across many unusual objects. Perhaps when discussing what sharks will eat, it would be better to consider what they won't eat. Basically, of course, the larger sharks are an effective "fish-eating machine", their diet mainly consisting of fish, mammals and other marine animals. Being the killers of the old and the weak, they carry out an important task of "culling down" large schools of fish, since it is the sick and imperfect fish, the stragglers from the school, that

21

are eliminated. Only the strongest survive, and this in itself must play an important part in ensuring that only the best of the species are left for breeding purposes. During experimental work in open-ocean localities in the Central and South Pacific, I have often observed schools of pelagic fish, such as tuna, accompanied by one or more large sharks, always within striking distance, watching and waiting. Because sharks play an extremely important part in maintaining the ecological balance of the marine environment, we must find ways and means of keeping the man-eating sharks at bay, rather than aiming at the wholesale and indiscriminate slaughter of the species.

Sharks also help to keep the oceans clean. The carcass of an animal, large or small, and no matter how rotten, is quickly devoured by these hungry predators. Every conceivable object found in the sea can at some time or other be recovered from the stomachs of sharks. While dissecting I have found the remains of sea-birds and seals, of turtles, stingrays, octopus, crayfish, sea urchins, starfish (including the venomous Crown of Thorns), pieces of coral, shell fish (including quite large clams), as well as a variety of other marine animals and even plants.

Once, I opened the stomach of a Tiger Shark and found an entire sea turtle weighing over a hundredweight, swallowed whole by the shark. None of the venomous or poisonous marine animals appears to dampen the appetite of a shark, for while examining one specimen I found two poisonous barbs from a stingray firmly embedded in its stomach wall. The shark appeared healthy, with a large and well-developed liver, always an accurate indication of their condition. It was obvious that the spines were having little or no effect on the feeding activities of the shark, which, in addition to the offending spines, had an assortment of fish pieces in its stomach.

The most unexpected things turn up in the innards of a shark: I have found beer cans and bottles, pieces of wood, including an entire butter box that had been flattened, cork and plastic floats, some with rope still attached, pieces of metal and wire, sometimes even rocks—as well as sacks, papers and pieces of cardboard. Once I found two cats inside a shark, these having been most likely dumped into the sea, for one had a piece of wire attached to its back leg just above the paw. On another occasion I found an army

22

boot still with the lace intact, as well as a wallet, which unfortunately was empty; and in another shark I found the propeller of an outboard motor.

A shark's gluttonous behaviour can be used against it, and some Pacific Island inhabitants have perfected a novel and effective way of catching sharks in large numbers. First the natives throw pieces of chopped-up fish into the water to attract the sharks. When a suitable number have arrived and commence to feed on the fish, the natives throw round jam (sometimes called pie) melons amongst the sharks. These melons have been heated in large copper-like cauldrons filled with boiling water. The outside shell prevents the contents from cooling when the melons are cast into the water, and the sharks quickly devour the offering, to their undoing. Once in the stomach of the shark the boiling interior of the melon soon kills its host and, because of the heat and the expanding gas in its stomach, the shark will eventually float up to the surface to be collected by the waiting fishermen.

Many strange cases have been recorded in which the destiny of men has been affected by objects removed from the stomach of a shark. Perhaps one of the most amazing incidents occurred in the West Indies, where the event is now referred to as the "Shark Papers". An American privateer operating against King George III's ships in the West Indies was finally cornered by a British man-o'-war. The captain, realizing that the game was up, threw his "Letters of Marque" and other ship's papers overboard before his ship was taken over by the British. He was subsequently taken for trial to Port Royal, Jamaica; but there was no documentary evidence against him and it appeared that he would be acquitted. But another British man-o'-war arrived in port with the American privateer's papers. The crew of the vessel had captured a large shark off the coast of Haiti, and when the scavenger's stomach was opened the missing papers were found still in a readable condition. The captain and crew of the privateer were condemned on this evidence. The original papers have been preserved and can still be seen at the Institute of Jamaica.

Another occasion when a shark affected people's lives was the famed "Shark Arm Case", which shocked Sydney during the year 1935. It all started when a fourteen-foot Tiger Shark tangled itself in shark lines and was captured alive and placed in the

Coogee Aquarium. After a week of captivity, during which time the Tiger refused all food, it suddenly disgorged several pieces of food it had eaten before it was captured. These were pieces of shark the Tiger had been attacking, a mutton bird, a rat—and a human arm. Police investigations revealed that the hand was in an excellent state of preservation and there was a tattooed picture of a boxer on the arm. Investigations proceeded, and it was soon established that the arm belonged to one James Smith. Doctors stated that the arm had been cut off the body, and not torn off by the shark, but a detailed search by police failed to find the rest of the body. After dramatic happenings, which included a newspaper's being sued for contempt of court, a high-speed chase in power boats on Sydney Harbour, a series of murder trials, rumours of a massive drug trafficking operation, and a conspiracy to defraud an insurance company of a vast amount of money, the case was finally closed without a solution being found to one of the strangest cases in the annals of crime.

There are many fallacies about the way in which a shark approaches its prey and bites. The most noteworthy of these is the old wives' tale that a shark must first turn on its back or side to eat, because of the undersnout position of the jaws and mouth. The truth of the matter is that a shark can eat in any position, and often gulps down food whole rather than use its teeth to cut it. It is fortunate indeed that sharks are generally cautious in approaching their food; for if this was not the case it would be impossible for a human to set foot in the ocean with safety, so numerous are the sharks. Usually sharks carefully survey the object to be eaten, gradually moving closer, perhaps circling the food. Finally, when satisfied, the shark moves in confidently, often in a rapid attack run and, immediately before seizing hold of its prey, brings the large pectoral fins on each side of its body into play as braking planes. Sharks can effortlessly slice great moon-shaped hunks of flesh from their prey; or, clamping their powerful jaws onto the victim, they use their weight together with a violent shaking and twisting motion of the body and head to tear the flesh apart and obtain a mouthful. It is this tearing motion that can be so disastrous when humans are attacked, for a shark can tear open a man's stomach and disembowel him while dragging and shaking to bite off a captured leg.

It is often argued that sharks are cruel and vicious killers, unmercifully slaughtering every living thing they encounter. This I cannot accept, even after being involved in a number of attacks, including the fatal mauling of young Ken. I don't hate sharks. I have no emotional attitude towards them. I respect them as perhaps the most perfectly adapted killers on this planet; but otherwise I see them as simply marine animals, a primitive form of life obeying basic instinctive patterns, killing humans as they kill fish—for food. I don't fear them, but I do respect them as the most powerful creatures known to man, totally unpredictable, and to be treated with extreme caution and watched as you'd watch a savage dog. The more I work with sharks and try to increase my knowledge of their behaviour, the less I seem to know. Although we have been successful in establishing general patterns of behaviour, there is always the exception to the rule, the one shark that will completely reverse the expected trend. Sharks are no crueller than any other predator in the sea.

The marine environment is a cruel world. From the very start of life in the planktonic community microscopic animal attacks and devours microscopic animal, in turn to be consumed by some larger form of life fighting the vicious and never-ending battle of survival. Small fish feed upon the minute life forms in the plankton, and they in turn are fed upon by large fish and other animals. And so on through the cycle to the sharks, the dominant predator of the oceans.

But the killing of one living thing by another form of life is the order of survival, with nothing being wasted in nature. Only man is the indiscriminate killer, slaughtering for material gain, for revenge, for lust or pleasure. Perhaps it is we who are the inhabitants of the cruel world and not the animals of the sea.

3

It is often stated that where there are porpoises or dolphins there will be no sharks. This unfortunately is not true, for I have seen sharks and porpoises together, working in harmony and rounding up the one school of fish, then feeding side by side. Perhaps not a common occurrence; but certainly sharks do not "fear" the presence of dolphins or porpoises. There is perhaps a mutual respect, and under normal conditions a "stand-off" exists; but I feel it is the sharks which have the advantage, for while examining their stomach contents I have often found the remains of porpoise and dolphin.

Occasionally a number of dolphins will attack a shark, repeatedly ramming its body with their sharply pointed snouts, causing injuries to its internal organs and finally killing it. This has been observed when a shark has threatened the young of a school of these warm-blooded mammals. Recently, Dr Perry Gilbert, now the Executive Director of the Mote Marine Laboratory at Sarasota in Florida, conducted a series of experiments with sharks and dolphins. Dolphins have been trained to attack and kill sharks in Dr Gilbert's well-equipped shark experimental pens. This research has been so successful that the project is to be carried a step further, and the trained dolphins taken to sea and there released to attack sharks on command. Soon, perhaps, it will be possible for divers on important scientific and military assignments to be protected from the dangers of shark attack by these highly intelligent and lovable animals.

It is not true that dolphins and porpoises are the fastest swimmers in the oceans. Since porpoises have been removed almost intact from the innards of large sharks, such as the White Shark and the Tiger, it is obvious that sharks are capable of even more tremendous bursts of speed. The famed underwater explorer, Hans Hass, judged their speed at between 40 and 70 knots! Many modern warships move at speeds in excess of 40 knots, and Hass claims that sharks have been seen to overtake these with ease. He has managed to get a few photographs of sharks under full steam. The blurring of the film allowed him to calculate the approximate speed of the creatures from the known shutter speed of the camera and the length of the shark. Such terrific speeds, even if possible, would only be maintained for a relatively short period, as in an attack run or in avoiding attack. The normal cruising speed of a shark would be very much slower.

The shark's main means of progression through the water is by means of sinuous sculling movements of the body and tail. Forward locomotive thrust is derived from the caudal half of the body and tail, as it swings from side to side. When sharks are swimming both the mouth and gills are open and a current of water passes over the gills. The fins are used as steering, balancing and braking devices and aids for sudden and violent movements. For speed, the shape of a shark is perfect, the body being beautifully streamlined to "torpedo" through the water.

While working at Rangiroa Atoll in the South Pacific I have often seen sharks hovering in the strong current that rushes into the lagoon through the narrow entrance pass. Here at times the rip exceeds ten knots, and the sharks appear to remain motionless as they hold their position effortlessly against the surging mass of water. I have seen them suddenly accelerate with incredible speed against this rushing torrent of water, to disappear with an effortless grace that is quite astounding.

While diving out in the crystal-clear waters of the open ocean several miles from Rangiroa, with the sea floor thousands of feet below, I had an experience of just how fast a shark could move. I was working at about ninety feet, adjusting the transducer (underwater loudspeaker) in preparation for an experiment in deep-water sound transmission. I checked the surrounding waters and found these clear. On looking up from the equipment no more than one or two seconds later to adjust the cable assembly, I came face to face with a large Tiger Shark only a few feet away, almost motionless and silently observing me. It must have approached at an incredible speed, and had it intended to attack I would have known nothing. Perhaps an outstanding characteristic of attacks on humans in our coastal waters, particularly those involving skin and Scuba divers, is that the attacking shark is rarely, if ever, seen before it strikes. An exception to this rule was my first serious encounter with a shark at Woodman's Point, Western Australia, during March 1956.

I had started diving and exploring the sea off the Western Australian coast during my early teens, following a move from Sydney to Perth to complete my schooling. I had always had a love of the ocean, of the cry of the seagulls, of the salt spray and the gleaming yellow sands. With the introduction of self-contained underwater breathing equipment in the early 1950s I became fascinated by the beauty of the underwater world. I lived for the weekends and holidays when, with my boyhood friends, I could explore its wonders. So enchanted did I become that I started work as a diver, and had as my tutors such men as the American, Tom Snider, owner of the flourishing Universal Salvage Company in Fremantle, and Ernie Ruttle, a former Royal Navy war-time frog-man hero, much decorated, who moved to Western Australia to take up dentistry. Both men have since died (Tom was killed in an aircraft crash during the 1960s), but they imparted much to me of their knowledge and experience of the ocean and its mysteries.

I saw my first large shark as a boy while spearfishing at Rott-nest Island, which is roughly about fifteen miles off the coast from Perth. A group of us had been spearfishing off the area known as the Narrow-neck, and I was leading the swimmers ashore, with the added thrust of a pair of "super-size" flippers. Suddenly, to my astonishment, my companions swam past me, and as the last of the group drew level he pointed behind. I turned and to my horror saw a large shark following a few yards away. With my flippers to add speed, I was waiting on the rocky shore when my exhausted spearfishing friends arrived, and together we gave our estimates of the size of the shark we had seen. These ranged from a respectable 12 feet or so, to a monstrous 30 feet or more.

In those early days of diving we had no wet suits, nor the money to purchase the expensive dry-type diving dress; but we dived winter and summer along the coast. During the winter our diving time was restricted to a mere thirty minutes or so at a time, after which we would stagger ashore, remove our sodden woollen jumpers and pullovers, and stand shivering between two huge fires lit on the beach. These were happy days, perhaps the best of my diving career, when everything was new and exciting and we were the explorers and the conquerors of this strange new world. Our friends, particularly the girls, would listen spellbound while we described our exploits, often grossly exaggerated as we told of giant sharks, huge fish, hidden wrecks and underwater caverns.

Diving around the Western Australian coast I was soon encountering many sharks, and I formed the opinion that they were mainly curious, and certainly not aggressive. I came to believe that a diver was immune from attack, and that only a swimmer was in danger, since a person on the surface presented an attractive target to a prowling shark. I reasoned that sick, injured, and dead fish invariably went to the surface of the water, and that a shark would associate anything there with weakness. Sharks loved octopus, and a swimmer moving along the silvery ceiling of the underwater world looked remarkably like an octopus, with legs and arms waving about as he moved through the water. It appeared to me that sharks became particularly forward in their approaches, and far more interested in a diver when he attempted to leave the water than when he remained and faced them in their own domain.

In 1954 I enlisted in the Western Australian Police Force and established their first diving and rescue squad. It was in 1956, while still serving as a member of the force, that I decided to experiment with long-endurance dives with self-contained diving equipment. It was decided that I, with a close friend, John Lee, should attempt to establish a new world underwater endurance record. Since the Navy was interested in the outcome of the programme, approval was granted for me to use the Naval facilities at Woodman's Point about thirty miles south of Perth, and to use the jetty where conditions were ideal for the attempt.

On the second attempt at the record during March 1956, I

entered the water at 4.45 on a Saturday afternoon. I was employing a cut-down 44-gallon drum as an underwater "armchair". This had been filled with rocks and cement and had taken three divers considerable effort to manhandle into position on the sand flat in ten feet of water out from the side of the jetty. The drum was close to a decline in the sea-floor and at a point some yards in front of my "arm chair" the sand dropped away gently to a depth of about 40 feet. It was intended that I spend at least twenty-five hours under water without surfacing, to break the existing record of twenty-four hours that had been established in a heated tank in the United States. Food was no problem, for I had perfected a method of drinking hot soup and coffee under water with ease. A thermos flask was fitted with a clamped rubber tube inserted through the sealing cork. My attendant divers would deliver me fresh hot soup or coffee at regular intervals. I merely unclamped the rubber tube, removed my aqualung mouthpiece and forced some compressed air into the flask. By tilting the flask the contents would be forced into my mouth. Between swallows I would take a breath of air and repeat the performance.

Much of my daylight hours was spent reading magazines and books while I sat in my "armchair". Although these became saturated immediately they were taken under water, and the pages would tear if any attempt was made to turn them by hand, I was able to overcome this problem. I found that by pulling the magazine or book gently through the water the resulting current would flick over just one page at a time without damaging the soft, sodden paper. With a little practice I soon became expert, and could flick through a magazine with as much ease as when on the surface. When I became bored with reading, I always had "George" to keep me company, a small sand whiting that had taken up residence beneath the 44-gallon drum and soon became quite tame, allowing me to stroke the side of his silvery-white body as he pecked at small pieces of vegetable soup I let escape into the water. As darkness approached and the soft twilight faded and dimmed my underwater world, "George" retreated to his quarters beneath the drum, evidently satisfied with his several hours of fossicking. I turned on my powerful underwater searchlight, constructed with a waterproofed sealed beam and powered from a generator on the Naval jetty. With the aid of the strong beam of light I spent the next hours fascinated by the marine life the light attracted. I was soon surrounded by hundreds of squid of varying sizes, which danced in the soft illumination at each side of the beam. Their iridescent bodies flashed with every colour of the rainbow as they approached quite close to me, completely unafraid of this strange apparition that had invaded their domain. Numerous small white sea-worms floated about close to the beam, and propelled themselves with short, jerky movements. One attempted to corkscrew down through the coarse fibres of my heavy woollen gloves when I held my fingers to the light.

At about 9 p.m. I received the attentions of another visitor, this time an unwelcome one: for silhouetted in the gloom at the extreme range of my searchlight I saw a shark. I immediately released my shark alarm buoy to warn those above on the jetty of the impending danger. A system of three buoys, anchored under water to the side of my drum, had been devised. When released, they bobbed to the surface where they were readily visible to my assistants. Yellow was to signal that I wished a diver to attend, perhaps for food or some other reason, White was the buoy indicating that I needed urgent assistance, and Red was for shark-attack danger.

I was armed with a powerful compressed-air speargun, the best on the market at that time, as well as several spare air cylinders capable of releasing a blast of highly compressed air. These were used to scare off sharks on a number of occasions during my diving career. I decided to use the compressed air, and held the shark in the beam of light as I fully opened the valve on the cylinder. The air hissed out with a thunderous roar, and as I fought to hold the wildly pitching cylinder in my grasp I was enveloped in a swirling mass of foaming air bubbles. I lost sight of the shark in the cauldron of foam, and this did nothing to ease my state of mind. The water quickly cleared, and on examining my surroundings with the light I found that the shark had left. I waited some minutes before winding in the shark alarm buoy, which was the agreed to "all clear" signal. No sooner had this been done than John Lee was at my side and wrote on the slate we used to communicate between divers, "We could see the shark from the jetty in the beam of your light. It was big." This news further unnerved me, but I decided to carry on with the attempt, hoping that the shark would not return.

31

Later in the night two divers arrived with fresh soup. They waited until I had finished and then left, taking the thermos with them. I could hear their departure through the water as they surfaced near the jetty and splashed about, no doubt hoping the commotion they were creating would scare off any sharks that were lurking in the vicinity. Shortly afterwards, at 11.55 p.m.—I was wearing an underwater watch and had just checked the time—I was sitting in the drum patrolling the waters ahead with my powerful light. Suddenly there was an unnatural quiet, a hush that spread through the water. A silence so profound I have never known before or after. It was as though all the world stood still, all things holding their breath for just a second or two to witness what was about to happen. I remember I could hear my heart pounding in my chest, and my blood rushing through the arteries and veins in my body with an audible swishing. For some reason I will never know, I turned the light to the right side of the drum in time to see a huge shark charging down on me. I could see its teeth as its jaw opened. It looked so unreal, so huge and terrifyingly out of proportion, as it bore down on me. I don't remember acting, even moving, but I must have fired my compressed air gun off at point-blank range, for later I learnt that I had scored a direct hit. Everything seemed to explode about me and I was flung sideways through the water. There was a terrible roar as if I was under the wheels of an express train; then it suddenly faded and there was nothing. I was lying flat on my back on the sand, and could see the light tracing a crazy pattern to the surface from where it, too, had fallen. I was still breathing. I could hear my air bubbles racing madly upwards. I could dimly see my drum chair lying on its side a few feet away. Terror seized me, and I flung myself across the sand to the drum and frantically tore at the cords securing the emergency floats. I dared not surface, for once there I was sure that I would be attacked again. I crouched by my drum in the darkness and felt with outstretched hand for the flex of my light. By some miracle I was able to locate this and thankfully pulled over the sealed beam. This gave me a measure of confidence, for at least I could see.

After what seemed an eternity but was in fact just a few moments John was at my side again with two or three other divers. Later they said that all three buoys had exploded to the surface together and they knew something serious had happened. John was to tell me later that when they reached the drum the scene resembled a battlefield, with pieces of equipment littered about on the sand. It must have taken considerable courage for John and the other divers to enter those dark forbidding waters armed only with weak torches. We crouched together on the sand by the drum, not knowing what to do. My gun had gone, vanished into the darkness. I suddenly became aware of cold water in my suit, spreading its icy fingers and chilling my warm body. To protect me from the penetrating cold of the surrounding water during my record attempt, I was wearing a heavy-duty, rubber, dry diving suit and hood, under which I had six pairs of heavy long-sleeved and long-legged woollen underwear. An assortment of jumpers and pullovers as well as heavy woollen socks and gloves completed my attire. All of this was kept bone dry by the suit, apart from the gloves. I advised John that I was wet, and together we examined the suit with the aid of the underwater torches carried by the divers. In the right leg of the suit was a gaping hole, through which protruded torn woollen underwear. After this discovery it was obvious that I must surface, because my suit was rapidly filling with water. At about 12.30 on the Sunday morning I thankfully left the water and climbed up onto the jetty.

John could see that I had been completely unnerved by my experience; so the following morning he insisted that I re-enter the water and help the other divers locate my gun and retrieve the rest of my equipment. This soon helped me to overcome my fears, and shortly afterwards, having recovered the equipment, I joined the other divers in the exhilarating pastime of riding a bucking cylinder of air. We would clutch a full tank of air between our legs, open the valve, and be jetted backwards through the water.

I was pleased when I visited the overturned drum the following morning and found "George" waiting patiently there. I showered the surrounding water with a generous supply of vegetable soup to show my appreciation of his loyalty. The drum was left where it had fallen, and "George" was still there when I departed later during the day.

My compressed air speargun was found at the bottom of the slope some considerable distance from the drum. The barrel of the gun, which was constructed of heavy metal similar to the barrel of a rifle, had been bent almost at right angles. The spear was recovered some considerable distance farther out from the jetty in forty feet of water; and although this was constructed of 3/8-inch high tensile spring steel it too had been bent at right angles. The strength of the spear was such that none of the divers present could bend the metal with their hands, even after placing one end into a crack in the jetty planking. The heavy spear barb, which had screwed onto the shaft of the spear, was missing and was never recovered. The astounding thing about this was that instead of the barb snapping off at the thread on the shaft, the steel of the shaft itself had been corkscrewed around and wrenched apart as though it had been in some gigantic metal press.

It was obvious what had happened. I had indeed scored a direct hit on the shark, and so close was the target at the time of firing that the spear did not have sufficient room to clear the barrel before it thudded into the shark's head. The shot had evidently knocked the shark off course, because it had crashed headlong into the drum, knocking this yards along the sand. As it swept past, the teeth of the shark had torn open the leg of my suit. It was only the six pairs of heavy woollen underwear that had saved me from serious injury. The heavy drum the three divers had so laboriously positioned had been flicked aside by the impact and was denuded of its silver paint on the right side, apparently at the point of impact. The slate we had used was recovered, the slate itself untouched but the wooden frame shattered into numerous pieces.

After this incident I lost my enthusiasm for night diving. But soon the horror of the attack faded to a dim memory as I resumed my underwater pursuits with as much vigour as before.

In 1957 I resigned from the Western Australian Police Force to form my own diving and salvage company. For the next year or so I worked the numerous wrecks that littered the western coast, salvaging scrap metal and whatever else was commercially usable. It was necessary to make extensive use of explosives for underwater blasting during this period, and I soon learnt that underwater explosions attracted sharks. After each blast sharks would soon arrive on the scene, nosing through the still discoloured waters surrounding the wreck site. While working on a Dutch submarine, the *K 35*, which had been wrecked in action during the

Second World War and then finally towed in and abandoned in shallow water at Woodman's Point, it was necessary to detonate a particularly large underwater explosion. The resulting blast had stunned a large school of skipjack (trevally) which, unknown to me, had been swimming close to the wreck. These now littered the sea floor surrounding the submarine and numbered several hundred. As I entered the water to examine the effects of the blast, a large shark appeared and cut a path through the fish lying on the sand. The shark merely opened its mouth like a huge scoop and gathered up the fish as it swam along.

Many of the wrecks I worked dated from the late nineteenth century and before. I remember salvaging huge cast-iron water pipes from the *Denton Holme*, which was wrecked on the coast of Rottnest Island in the late 1800s, and while doing so I made an interesting discovery. The *Denton Holme* was wrecked during a storm the night it reached the Western Australian coast after the long journey from England. The ship was bound for Fremantle, fifteen miles away. Someone on Rottnest Island lit a huge beacon to warn shipping away from the treacherous reefs that sent jagged fingers of rock far out into the sea from those surrounding the island. The approaching *Denton Holme* mistook the beacon for that marking the Port of Fremantle, and the vessel crashed head-long onto the reef close to Thompson Bay. Before that night was to pass another two overseas ships were to be lured to their destruction by the same beacon, with heavy loss of life.

I found the *Denton Holme* resting in about thirty feet of water, close to the wrecks of the *Janet* and the *Transit*, for Rottnest Island is a graveyard of ships. On working down through the decks of the wreck I came upon a hold that contained an assortment of items including a number of bottles, some in cases still intact, together with a quantity of clay-pipes, still usable and bearing the maker's name. I gathered a number of the bottles together and took these to the surface. Some I found contained stout, "White Horse" brand of Cork and Dublin, while other bottles contained genuine Jamaican rum, the markings being burned onto the inside of the corks sealing the bottles. Most of the stout was rotten, and the bottles would explode from time to time after they had been placed on the deck and were relieved of the surrounding water pressure. But a few, protected by the lead seal that encased the cork, were still effervescent and drinkable—a delicious beverage after seventy-eight years under the ocean. The rum was perfect, thick as syrup and with a kick like a mule. My diving apprentice, young Andy Cassidy, suggested we take some of the brew to the Rose Hotel, where his father was the head barman. A tough waterside hotel, frequented by sailors and waterside workers, the Rose proved to be an ideal market for the rum. Dan opened a bottle and poured a nip to some of his customers who lined the bar. There followed much smacking of lips and the orders flowed in—so much so that the demand soon exceeded the very limited supply.

When I visited Perth I would always stay at Leederville with old Mrs Dancer, affectionately known to one and all as "Gran". Gran's kitchen was soon well stocked with cups and plates and the other assorted galley utensils I salvaged from time to time from the wrecks I explored.

I also spent considerable time searching for the *Gilt Dragon*, the fabled Dutch treasure ship that was wrecked in 1656 on the Western Australian coast close to Lancelin Island. Included amongst the cargo was 76,500 gold guilders, valued today at over several million dollars. With Harry Turner, who lived at Bassendean, a suburb of Perth, I undertook an extensive survey of the Lancelin Island-Ledge Point area, where we knew the vessel had been wrecked. Copies of the original charts made by the commanders of the Dutch vessels that had searched for survivors of the *Gilt Dragon* for three years after the wreck were obtained from the archives at the Hague. With Ted Packer and his aircraft (Ted was a friend from my own flying days) we made an aerial survey of the locality, photographing the outline of the coast and comparing this with the Dutch charts made more than 300 years before. These proved to be remarkably accurate, and we were able to identify a number of landmarks, including reefs and islands. But the search proved unsuccessful and the project had to be abandoned.

Ted was a wonderful pilot, and we had flown together for a number of years. At one stage during my police career I had tried to induce the Police Department to enlarge the scope of my activities to include those of air-police, since I was then flying with the Perth Royal Aero Club. This proposal was well ahead of its time, and the suggestion was promptly rejected by the department.

36

This did not stop Ted from helping me—and the Police Department—in my rescue activities on many occasions with considerable success.

After the unsuccessful search for the *Gilt Dragon* I tried to locate the *Sepia*, which foundered late in the nineteenth century between Carnac and Rottnest islands off the coast from Fremantle. She was carrying amongst her cargo 100 tons of mercury, with a present-day value of around two million dollars. This too remained an elusive goal and lack of funds forced the abandonment of the search.

The *Sepia* (an iron barque) has since been located a mile and a half west of Carnac Island and is resting on the seafloor of pure white sand. The wreck is now regularly visited by local divers and underwater enthusiasts, and for the collectors of antique bottles is proving most rewarding. But the valuable cargo of mercury has not been found.

In 1957 I had bought the *Comet*, a gaff-rigged auxiliary ketch of 10 tons, from a newly established boat brokerage firm in Perth. Later this vessel was to be condemned as unseaworthy by the shipping authorities. The brokers had arranged for a certificate of seaworthiness to be issued by a surveyor of ill-repute. With no funds to begin legal proceedings—my file is still gathering dust in a Perth solicitor's office awaiting my pleasure to commence proceedings against the brokers—and a rapid decline in scrap metal prices, I was forced to wind up my diving business. I conducted some fish migratory surveys, including the "runs" of crayfish along the western coast, for several commercial fishing enterprises before leaving Australia for the Cocos-Keeling Islands. Later I enlisted in the Northern Territory Police Force, where I became that department's first police diver.

4

I spent many sleepless nights re-living the series of events leading up to the tragedy. I couldn't understand why the shark had struck when it did and not a few minutes before when both Ken and I had been so much more accessible in deep water well out from the shore. If the shark had followed the general rule of extreme caution in approaching its prey, it must have been in the immediate vicinity for some time before the attack. If I could establish the cause of the attack, this would help me in finding a shark repellent.

I reconstructed the scene: Two boys were splashing and playing in the water and by doing so were causing unusual vibrations to echo outwards, vibrations similar, I reasoned, to those emitted by a wounded fish. This was what had first excited and attracted the shark. Before the attack could take place the stimulus or attracting vibrations ceased: one of the boys left the water. Then followed several minutes of even, relaxed swimming with no unusual sound impulses, while Ken and I swam leisurely out into mid-stream and back, employing a relaxed form of breast stroke. The victim, Ken, again began to splash and play about close inshore, again making the sound signals that echoed outward through the water. The waiting shark then responded to these vibrations and attacked.

This, I thought, was what probably happened. But I still had my doubts, for I had read and heard that a good defence against shark attack was to splash and thump the water so that the commotion would scare off any sharks. Hans Hass claimed that he only had to "bark like a dog" under water and the resulting sound would send sharks hurrying on their way. Others said that an effective defence was to scream beneath the surface; and I myself had employed a high-pressure jet of compressed air to scare off sharks. Perhaps, I thought, the sharks might soon become accustomed to sudden loud noises and then cease to fear them. I had always expected to see a shark, sometimes several, after the spearing of a large fish: within a minute or two they would be there, circling around and looking for the fish. But, again, they may have been responding to the blood spilled from the speared fish, and not to the struggling that followed.

I knew that sharks had good vision, despite reports to the contrary. After being attacked at Woodman's Point I became for a time very shark conscious. Instead of looking for the animals in the immediate vicinity, I used to search the region at the very limits of my vision where the surrounding gloom concealed the underwater landscape from my sight. Here I had sensed the presence of sharks, and would soon be rewarded with a shadowy outline, just a fleeting glimpse of some large animal as it moved majestically through the water at the extreme limit of my vision. Even when I froze I would sometimes continue to see the sharks as they maintained their distant inspection of my presence. I was sure that the animals could see me clearly, though I could not see them, for their sight had been adapted by aeons of evolution to the environment. I would say that a shark can see half the distance again that a man armed with facemask can see when he dives under water. Sight, therefore, must play an important role in the feeding behaviour of a shark, but only where the clarity of the water enables the animal to employ his visual apparatus.

Sometimes sharks seem to have been guided to their victims purely by colour. An interesting though tragic case relates to the ditching of a military aircraft in the tropical regions of the Pacific. Following the crash, the crew was forced to take to the water with life jackets. Some were dressed in flying suits of a bright orange colour; others were clothed in flying suits of a green material. All those in the orange were subsequently slaughtered by shark attacks, and only the flyers dressed in green were rescued.

I knew that I could dismiss sight as the agent that led to the fatal shark attack on young Ken. The water had been so murky it had been difficult to see more than a foot or so at the most, and no matter how efficient a shark's vision its sight could have played no part in those conditions.

Sharks have a keenly developed sense of smell. There is evidence that, with a suitable water current moving from the source of the stimulus, a shark can detect an odour such as blood or fish oil from over a quarter of a mile. It has been established that sharks can detect an attractive olfactory stimulus, such as blood, when this has been diluted to a concentration of 1 part to 1.5 million parts of water.

Study of the anatomy of a shark's brain shows a high degree of development of the regions associated with the sense of smell. This, together with the intricate system of folds in the nostrils, leaves little doubt that smell also plays an important part in the everyday life of a shark.

Certain attacks on humans could perhaps be attributed to olfactory stimulus that has drawn a shark to its prey. Take, for instance, a crowded beach with dozens or even hundreds of persons in the water. There are records of attacking sharks moving through and among bathers, even pushing people aside, to get to their selected target. It is possible that some people, perhaps as the result of a recent cut or wound, or even perhaps from their body odour, are more attractive than others to sharks.

But I could dismiss olfactory stimulus in the attack on Ken, for if this had been the cause surely the shark would have struck when its target was so much more accessible in deep water well out from the shore? Ken had no cuts or wounds, and I knew that he and other boys had often swum in the same place.

The "hearing" apparatus of a shark or the lateralis system, more commonly known as the lateral line, is extremely well developed. The system comprises a series of fine canals or channels along each side of the head, circling its orbits and following the line of the jaws, and running down almost the entire length of each side of the body.

These canals or channels are located just beneath the outer skin in the deeper layers and are filled with a watery solution or mucus. The canals are connected to the outer surface of the skin at intervals through tubules or pores. There are clusters of sensory cells, called neuromasts, along the inner surface of the canals. From these sensory cells bunches of tiny hair-like processes reach into the fluid that fills the canals. Vibrations or sound waves reaching the outer skin openings of the tubules act upon the mucus. This fluid transmits the vibrations along the tubules into the canals where they are registered and transformed into nerve impulses by the special cells in the canal walls. The sensory cells then communicate the impulses to the animal's brain.

In addition to the hearing ability of the lateralis system, it seems probable that from the strength of the signals received a shark is able to judge their origin and distance. This enables it to locate its prey quickly and accurately in water too murky for its visual apparatus to guide it. The lateralis system could also be called a shark's "direction finder".

Recent research indicates that in addition to lateral line reception the shark also "hears from the top of its head". At Eniwetok Atoll in the Central Pacific during August of 1972 Professor Al Tester and three associates from the University of Hawaii carried out experiments on the hearing apparatus of sharks, and the data obtained suggested that a shark is also receptive to sound vibrations received through a sensitive area on the top of the head. This seems to constitute a unique and remarkably sensitive hearing system.

I became convinced that sound vibrations from Ken's splashing and playing in the water led to the attack. But this remained to be proved, and to test my theory I commenced a series of experiments shortly after my arrival on Magnetic Island in North Queensland. The result was a scientific paper entitled, "Swimmers in Distress and the Related Effect on the Behaviour Pattern of Sharks". I used the term "distress" to designate any unusual commotion in the water: splashing and playing about, any jerky or violent movement, panic-stricken behaviour, or the motions of drowning. The initial experiments were conducted in the many secluded bays around the island which at that time abounded in sharks. The results were later confirmed in New Guinea and elsewhere. As the waters on the eastern and northern sides of the island were then crystal clear and inviting, being free from the silt pollution that was later to invade the area from the Harbour Board dredge activities, it was easy to obtain visual records of each experiment.

These tests were not without danger, and on a number of occasions I experienced some hair-raising moments. The object was to establish whether a swimmer in "distress" transmitted sound frequencies or vibrations that would alter the general behaviour pattern of sharks, making them more aggressive towards the swimmer. Various sharks were encounted during the course of the programme, including the Whaler Shark, the Bronze Whaler, the Tiger Shark, and the smaller White-tip and Black-tip Reef Sharks.

I conducted the experiments at various times during daylight hours, and found that I achieved the best results at the period of slack water dûring full tide. Results were also more favourable at low tide during slack water than when the tide was in flood, that is, during the rise and fall of the tide. The method I employed was simple. Once I had selected the test site, this being continually varied, I would enter the water. Often sharks would already be in visual range, and I would commence to transmit "distress stimulus" through my body movements and then record the subsequent reactions of the test animals. The effect was generally to excite the shark into making a closer inspection of the source of the unusual vibrations or signals, and at first I found this most disconcerting. Fortunately the sharks that frequented Magnetic Island's waters at that time had good "table manners", and the area had been free from attacks for over thirty years. An abundance of natural food in the way of fish was available and the sharks had little cause to be interested in anything else. As soon as I stopped my thrashing about in the water the sharks would lose interest and move away.

I used to remain as still as possible and watch the sharks while they remained in visual range. After a shark had been lost completely from sight, I was often able to "call in" the animal again simply by recommencing the distress stimulus; but on these occasions the sharks would become more aggressive towards me, and I decided once was enough.

The sharks seemed to adopt typical patterns of approaching me. Some would commence to circle me in the water, gradually reducing the radius of the circle and making closer inspection sweeps. Sometimes a shark would move in a circular pattern some distance away to evaluate a possible meal. Sometimes sharks would make fast, agitated and jerky movements, and I would launch myself out of the water and into my waiting dinghy, where I would fall in an undignified heap, swearing that that was the finish of the project: I knew that these movements were the prelude to the attack run.

The transmission time of the distress stimulus varied from a few seconds to several minutes or more, and its strength depended on my physical condition and capabilities. Of the 103 tests conducted while a shark or sharks were already in attendance and in visual contact before I began the transmission of distress stimulus, a positive result was obtained in 78. When no sharks were to be seen in the vicinity, 129 out of the 282 experiments were successful in attracting or calling in one or more sharks to me. If I remained completely inactive when the shark first approached it generally lost interest almost immediately and would disappear. Even the smaller, docile species of shark, the reef varieties, could be excited to make a closer inspection as I danced about in the water like a crazy puppet on a string. Only once did I get a real fright, and this was when a Tiger Shark about 11 feet in length came charging out of the surrounding gloom straight towards me. I froze and remained perfectly still, hardly daring to breathe, and after a short time, and much to my relief, the shark disappeared from sight.

The results of this programme established conclusively that any swimmer who behaves in an excited, unusual or panic-stricken manner in the water transmits through his movements sound frequencies or vibrations that can call in or attract sharks. It was obvious that in turbid or discoloured water the dangers of shark attack would be greatly increased for anyone in the water behaving in this manner, because the shark would be responding to attractive sound stimulus and might attack without making visual contact with its prey.

I took the project a step further, and was able to establish that the safest way of moving through the water in the vicinity of a shark or sharks, was to employ a relaxed form of breast stroke or frog kick as this is often called. Any swimming stroke that involved the lifting of any part of the arms or hands, legs or feet above the surface of the water was distinctly dangerous and should be avoided, for the resulting splashing, even if of a rhythmic pattern, could still excite a shark to take an interest in the swimmer. Obviously the safest thing to do when confronted by a shark is to remain perfectly still, observing the animal. If it becomes necessary to move through the water, the safest method is to use a slow, relaxed form of breast stroke. The so-called butterfly stroke, which I nicknamed the "suicide stroke", is particularly effective in attracting sharks to the swimmer.

Once I had established beyond any doubt that sound was the agent responsible for Ken's attack, and indeed was most likely the main factor in a majority of the shark attacks in our coastal regions, I reasoned that if it played such an important part in attracting sharks to their prey, perhaps the reverse would apply: perhaps sound could be used to repel sharks.

Since all the known and reputed man-eating species of shark appeared to respond to the same basic sound frequencies that had the ability to attract or call them in to the target, I believed that the underwater transmission of certain sound frequencies would quickly provide the much desired answer. But I was soon to learn that there was no quick answer to the problem of finding an all-purpose shark repellent. And so started a detailed, expensive, extremely complex, and often most frustrating research undertaking that is still continuing.

The sharks considered dangerous to man have to be divided into two classes, the known man-eaters and the reputed man-eaters. The known man-eating species of shark are few. Of these, the White Shark (*Carcharodon carcharias*), is the most ferocious and dangerous known to man. Often called by Australians the White Pointer, this shark is also known throughout the rest of the world under a variety of names which include the White Death, the Great White Shark, the Grey Shark, the Grey Death and the Grey Pointer. Without a doubt this is the most terrible monster the seas have produced in recent times. It has been recorded to a length of almost 40 feet, with a specimen of $39\frac{1}{2}$ feet being captured off the Hawaiian Islands in the late 1930s, and another estimated at $36\frac{1}{2}$ feet in length at Port Fairy in Victoria. Such an animal must have weighed several tons or more. The White Shark is found in every ocean and sea of the world. It is most prolific in cooler waters, although still common and often encountered in tropical and semi-tropical regions.

Since men first took to the sea in ships the White Shark has been known and feared, instilling terror into the most hardy of sailors. Perhaps the "ghostly" white appearance of this huge shark has earned it its evil reputation, for there is something unreal and sinister about the great beast. The White Shark has been known to follow sailing vessels for days, even weeks, gliding silently near the keel or close to the stern, watching and waiting. It has been recorded in the old sailing days that the hungry monster has reached out of the ocean to snatch some helpless seaman from the side of his becalmed ship.

On the few occasions when I have encountered this terrible animal under water, I have always been impressed by its unnatural appearance. It has a huge unblinking black eye, and is easily identified by its mackerel-shaped tail—in fact the family Isuridae which comprises the White Shark and its near relative the Blue Pointer or Mako Shark (*Isurus glaucus*), also a reputed man-eater, are often known as the Mackerel Sharks. It has been said that if a diver comes face to face with a White Shark this is the last thing he will ever see. But like the Lion, the Lord of the Jungle, these sharks have been known to turn and flee in terror at the sight of a man under water. It is enough to know that this huge beast attacks without provocation and without warning, and that it has devoured many of the hapless victims of disasters at sea. It is fortunate that the White Shark is a pelagic species, roaming the deep ocean waters of the world and only rarely entering the shallow waters of our coastal regions. There is a recorded case of one of the old sailing clippers being attacked repeatedly by this huge animal while moving through the sea. When, a few weeks later, the vessel was run onto the slip for careening, there, embedded deeply in the timbers, having penetrated the stout copper sheathing, was the entire jaw of a White Shark. So furious had been the animal's attack, and so powerful its bite that it had been unable to withdraw its teeth.

The White Shark is the only shark that appears to be capable of a basic and limited reasoning. It is the only shark that will retaliate immediately if molested or injured, its other relatives usually showing a desire to escape rather than attack. When I have captured these huge animals on the massive set rig employed for the pelagic sharks, I have seen them attack and sink the 44-gallon drums used as marker buoys. When brought alongside

45

they have attacked the side of the boat, and on one occasion an angry White Shark smashed the divers' platform on the stern of the boat to splintered matchwood, all the time making the most terrible growling and grunting noises.

Another known man-eater is the Whaler Shark (*Carcharhinus leucas*), which is the species responsible for the majority of attacks in Australian waters. A friend of mine, Professor Jack Garrick, of the Wellington University, New Zealand, and a world authority on sharks, has discovered in recent years that the dangerous Zambesi Shark of South Africa, the feared Bull Shark of the United States, and the species responsible for human attacks in the Tigris and Euphrates rivers and in the Ganges and other rivers and streams of India and Pakistan, is none other than *Carcharhinus leucas*. And the aggressive fresh-water sharks of Lake Nicaragua and Lake Izabal in Guatemala, as well as at least one lake in New Guinea, are also Whaler Sharks. This dangerous animal inhabits close inshore waters, including tidal harbours, rivers, streams, creeks and estuaries, where its favourite haunts include brackish backwaters. It lurks in the often turbid water, unseen, but an everpresent menace. It was a shark of this species that fatally mauled Ken.

Growing to a length of around 14 to 15 feet, this shark is often found in regions of completely fresh water, so far does it move upstream from the sea and tidal influence. During experimental work with the Whaler Shark and its close relative the Bronze Whaler (*Carcharhinus ahenea*), I have found that these animals must be treated with extreme caution and respect. Although the Bronze Whaler is reputed to be a man-eating shark, the largest of this species I have ever encountered was around 7½ to 8 feet in length. Certainly the animal is a very lively one, and also a very beautiful one when observed in its natural habitat. Unlike the Whaler Shark, the Bronze Whaler is to be found only in the clear open sea of the coastal regions. Its bright bronze colouring, lightening to a pure white underneath the body, is very attractive to behold.

Another of the known man-eating sharks that has earned its evil reputation around the entire globe is the Tiger (*Galeocerdo cuvieri*). More common in the tropical and sub-tropical regions than in cooler waters, these sharks are universally known and feared. Estimated to reach a size of at least 30 feet, this species is identifiable when seen under water by the distinctive stripes that have earned it the name of "Tiger". These stripes become less noticeable as the shark grows larger, and the markings tend to blend in with the surrounding colouring. Even in a small shark they fade quickly after death. The species was tentatively identified as the one responsible for the fatal mauling of Robert Bartle, 23 years, of Perth, when he was bitten completely in half while spear-fishing in clear waters north of Jurien Bay, during August 1967. The shark, previously unseen by the victim or his companion witness, suddenly rushed upon Bartle and seized his body in its jaws, severing it at a point inches below the rib-cage, and swallowing the buttocks and legs whole. The horrified witness to this terrible incident was Lee Warner, of Perth. He told of seeing the attacking shark's eye roll white, as if it was covered with white skin, when the animal flashed past him. In this Warner would have been referring to the nictitating membrane, which is sometimes called a third eyelid. This is a protective whitish membrane of tough skin that slides up over the eye of the shark when it attacks. Not all species have this. It is absent in the White Shark, but the Tiger has it. This evidence, together with an examination of the later recovered upper portion of the body, which revealed even teeth marks on the upper and lower surfaces corresponding to the upper and lower jaws of the shark, tentatively established that a Tiger Shark had been responsible for Bartle's death.

These three species are the most dangerous man-eaters known, and would be responsible for the majority of attacks and fatalities throughout the oceans of the world.

Included among the suspect sharks, or reputed man-eaters, are the larger Hammerheads, including *Sphyrna lewini*, with their oddly shaped heads and widely separated eyes, and the Great Blue Shark (*Prionace glauca*), another of the deep water or pelagic species. In the United States the Lemon Shark (*Negaprion brevirostris*), the Dusky Shark (*Carcharhinus obscurus*) and the Oceanic White-tip Shark (*Carcharhinus longimanus*) are all considered dangerous.

The famed Grey Nurse (*Carcharias taurus*) must be mentioned, too. This shark has been credited, although unjustly, by the Australian Press, with more attacks on humans than any other species. Perhaps there is something sinister in the name "Grey Nurse" which excites public interest. I have found the animal to be extremely docile and lethargic if left alone and unmolested, though it certainly has a frightening appearance, with a hideous array of long, awl-like teeth protruding from its ferocious-looking jaws. Generally, if approached quietly, it is too lazy to move off the sea floor where it appears to spend much of its life. There is no evidence that a Grey Nurse Shark has ever been involved in an attack on a human. But, as with all marine animals I encounter, I treat this one with the caution and respect it deserves.

A few of the harmless sharks warrant a mention, and these include the Whale or Checkerboard Shark (*Rhincodon typus*), which reaches the estimated length of a staggering 70 to 75 feet. This huge and gentle creature roams the oceans feeding on the plankton and minute fishes that nourish its enormous bulk. Another "monster" with an equally gentle disposition is the Basking Shark (*Cetorhinus maximus*), which also feeds on plankton and has been known to exceed 40 feet in length. Occasionally one of these huge sharks will be rammed by a passing steamer as it lazily moves about in the warm surface layers of the ocean.

Another shark of interest is the Thresher Shark (*Alopias vulpinus*) with its beautifully fashioned tail. This perhaps is one of the easiest sharks to recognize, since the upper lobe of the tail is as long if not longer than the rest of the body.

The unusual six and seven gilled sharks (most sharks have only five gill openings) I have seen in the shallow waters of a lagoon in the Central and South Pacific, but they appear to prefer the deeper waters of the ocean.

The many beautiful and often delicately marked reef species are ever present. They include the Wobbegong or Carpet Sharks, their multi-patterned bodies blending in with the surrounding environment to make them difficult to detect. These sharks are so fond of crayfish that they will actually enter a cray-pot to obtain these succulent marine delicacies. In Western Australia I once found a seven-foot specimen inside one of my standard cane cray-pots. So large was the Wobby that it occupied the entire inside of the pot, and it is still a mystery how it fitted itself down the narrow neck. I had to dismantle the pot to free the shark, which was later eaten with relish by members of my party.

The Grey Reef Shark, a known man-eater, swims dangerously close to the author at Rangiroa Atoll

Lagoon sharks fight over a captured fish in the maelstrom

The harmless and beautifully marked Epaulette Shark, one of the common
tropical reef varieties (it grows to a length of 3 to 4 feet)

A Wobbegong Shark (also called a Carpet Shark) peers out at the author
(its markings make it difficult to see)

The Whaler Shark, a known man-eater responsible for the majority of attacks
on humans in Australian coastal waters

Two sharks rest on the floor of a reef lagoon on the Great Barrier Reef

The aggressive White-tip Reef Shark, common in Rangiroa lagoon, becomes particularly dangerous when excited with distress stimulus

American expedition members lower the new shark cage into a boat for
the trip out to the maelstrom

Divers work to secure the cage on the lagoon floor

Sharks batter themselves to death and become jammed in a coral cave as
they attempt to reach the source of the distress stimulus signals

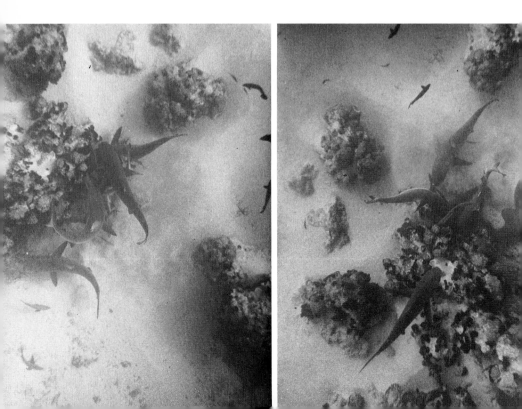

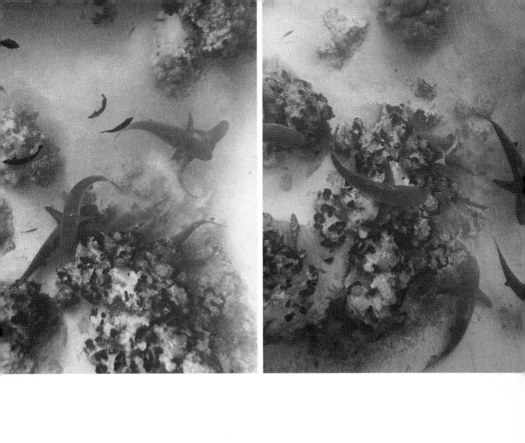

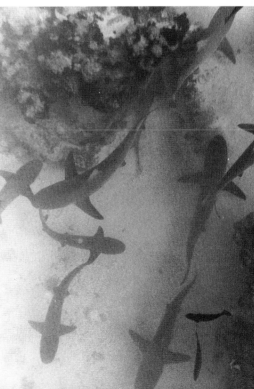

With the cage firmly secured, divers remove the inflatable bag (the cage is in 50 feet of water)

Robert swims up to the surface with a captured Grey Shark. Over 70 feet below is the floor of the entrance pass, swept clean by the rushing current

The underwater camera man records the gill and jaw movements of a resting Nurse Shark. Although reaching over 9 feet in length, these sharks are not dangerous to man

Tagging a shark before releasing it in the lagoon

The numbered, stainless steel tag is firmly attached with a special applicator

Dr Glen Egstrom swims down through the lagoon entrance pass at a depth of 70 feet

The author and trainee Stephen McLean prepare shark-catching equipment at Middle Harbour, Sydney

Trainee student research assistants Stephen McLean (*right*) and Robert Finch (*left*) examine a small Tiger Shark

The White-tipped and Black-tipped Reef Sharks, and the beautiful little Epaulette Shark, are just some of the host of wonderful animals that make up part of the family of sharks.

Sharks are of extreme benefit to mankind as a source of food, and anyone who has bought cooked fish or eaten it in a restaurant has no doubt eaten, and enjoyed, shark flesh. In Perth an experiment was conducted with the prepared flesh of several of the best eating fish, including Dhue-fish (Jew-fish) and Snapper as well as shark flesh. It was cooked in various ways and presented with a numbered identification marking only, to the gourmets who were participating in the experiment. None of those who ate the prepared flesh could distinguish between the other fish and the shark. The Chinese are fond of shark-fin soup made from the sun-dried fins, and shark hide is much in demand because it makes tough and good-looking leather from which to make shoes and boots, wallets, golf-bags, luggage, watchbands, and dozens of other useful objects. At one time the liver of sharks was much sought after because of its high Vitamin A content, and many fishermen were made rich through shark fishing before the introduction of synthetic Vitamin A put an end to the market.

5

The more I investigated the sonic approach to shark repellents the more I became convinced that here at last was the key to solving the problem. To be effective, any positive, all-purpose shark deterrent must be able to be applied at the commencement of the pattern generally adopted by a shark in approaching its intended prey. This general pattern had been established after exhaustive research by Dr Perry Gilbert and his associates.

At distances of between 100 and 200 metres (330 and 660 feet) from the target, the shark responds to vibrations or sound frequencies which it received through the auditory and lateralis system. Such would be the attractive stimulus emitted by a wounded fish, or a swimmer in distress, or one who was playing and splashing about in the water.

At closer distances, depending on the olfactory stimulus and the prevailing currents, the sense of smell is employed by the shark in directing it to its prey.

At closer distances again, the shark employs visual contact, but again this is dependent on the existing water conditions at the time. If the water clarity is such that the shark can utilise its visual apparatus, it makes final contact with its prey in this manner. However, often due to the turbid and murky water conditions existing during the attack run this cannot be done.

The important clue provided in this general attack pattern is that neither the olfactory nor the visual apparatus is essential to the shark in directing it to its target. The stimulus received by a shark in the form of distress signals (sound vibrations) is sufficient to allow contact to be made with the intended prey regardless of the olfactory stimulus and visual contact conditions existing at the time.

I was later to confirm this pattern through my own experimental work. A transducer (underwater loudspeaker) was set up on the sea floor where the water visibility was reduced to several feet. With a motion film camera, which had been set to expose only a limited number of frames each minute, and which was located directly behind the transducer, it was possible to monitor the test programme. Attractive sound vibrations were transmitted under water for limited periods, and it was established that these were effective in calling in the shark to the target, even though the animal could not make visual contact until the very last. As there was no attractive smell in the water to excite or guide the shark, it was obvious that the animal was "homing in" purely on the sound vibrations it was receiving.

When considering all the aspects of the general pattern adopted by sharks in approaching their victims, it became obvious to me that to be successful I would have to be able to repel the sharks at the very beginning of the intended attack. With this primitive form of life, subject to basic and instinctive patterns of behaviour, I reasoned that it would be extremely difficult, if not impossible, to deter the attacking shark once its approach to its prey had begun. If a suitable repellent could be used at the onset of this pattern, then no subsequent attack would be made. I then compiled an argument for and against the various possible ways of repelling sharks.

If an attempt was made to devise a repellent that could be used on the vision or sense of smell, the problems would be infinite. I had already seen the results of "Shark Chaser", which employed both these sensory systems, and I was not impressed. Admittedly these experiments had involved the frenzied feeding of sharks; but further tests had shown that even if "Shark Chaser" was applied well before the addition of the blood and offal that attracted the sharks it did not deter them from moving in and taking the set baits.

Experiments have been conducted with colour as a repellent, various shades being tried. Detailed tests have been made with a form of synthetic octopus ink together with numerous other dyes. Colour seems to make little difference where attacks on humans are concerned. In South Africa a white person was singled out from a group of natives on one day, and then a native was taken at almost exactly the same spot the next day. There is a strong belief that white attracts attention, and it may be true that sharks are attracted to a certain indefinable extent by lighter objects. A case in point was the mauling of the airmen dressed in bright orange, while those dressed in the duller green escaped uninjured. Coloured dyes could never be very effective with the sea so vast and for ever changing, so subject to currents and movements that would soon disperse any dye. And it is too much to hope that a hungry shark is going to turn aside from a meal merely because the surrounding water happens to be a darker or lighter shade than usual. The shark would already be well into its established attack pattern; and if the water conditions were such that visual contact between the shark and its intended victim could not be established, no such repellent could be employed. This would eliminate its successful application in areas of turbid or discoloured water, thus excluding most harbour areas, tidal rivers, and streams and estuaries, as well as badly discoloured ocean regions, such as surf beaches and the site of a disaster at sea. Sight is of little importance in the frenzied feeding of sharks: they will consume anything when in this state.

A repellent which relies on the sense of smell would in many cases not take effect until after the shark had commenced its initial approach. Even if a suitable repellent of this nature were found, it would be subject to such factors as the dilution rate in the surrounding water, the dissipation in currents, and the influence of weather conditions such as wind-produced drifts. No such repellent could hope to deter sharks during a frenzied state, when they appear to switch off their sensory systems involving sight and smell and respond only to sound frequencies or vibrations.

Could a repellent that relied on the shark's sense of hearing be used to protect man from the dangers of shark attack? A sound deterrent has distinct advantages over any other form of repellent, for it would take effect at the very start of the approach and before the shark had established its attack pattern. It would have considerable advantages over chemicals, poisons, irritants, stenches, dyes and shields. Sound would give instant protection and there would be no time lag such as would occur while the chemicals or dyes diffused around the swimmer. Sound would give a greater range of protection; it could be used intermittently to save power; it could be designed to work instantly on contact with water to protect the unconscious or stunned survivors of a disaster at sea.

The sonic approach to shark repellents could have an unlimited field of application. Through the underwater transmission of selected sound frequencies, harbours and beaches could be given year-round protection. It would only be necessary to establish a "sonic barrier" across the harbour entrance or between headlands bordering popular bathing beaches. This could be achieved by placing underwater transmitting units at selected intervals. These would be so designed that little maintenance was required, and an appropriate ultrasonic frequency would be incorporated in the signal pattern to inhibit the growth of marine organisms on the transmitting units. Power supplies would be maintained by special solar energy re-charging cells, secured above and on the surface by means of a floating buoy. The protective sonic barrier so formed would be safeguarded by placing the transmitting units in such a manner as to ensure an overlap of the signal pattern, so that in the event of a unit failing the barrier would be maintained. A monitoring system would automatically activate a warning device if the signal intensity dropped below the safe operational level through a fault in the equipment or any other cause. The sonic barrier so formed would not interfere with shipping activities and would not affect the bony fish life in the region. There would be no drastic reduction in the large predators frequenting any particular coastal locality, for the sonic barrier would repel and not eliminate. Many of the often beautiful waterways winding through the coastal cities and towns could be used for open public bathing once the danger from shark attack had been removed.

Although the combination of pure signal tones that will eventually provide the positive and lasting repellent signal to protect man from sharks is proving to be elusive, we already have the means of clearing harbours and rivers of the menace. Through the application of "distress stimulus", it is possible to remove all the sharks from any selected locality. They will follow the source of the attractive signals like a pack of dogs, and can be led well out to sea. Once the sonic repellent is perfected, the sharks can be cleared from the area to be protected, then a sonic barrier can be established across the harbour entrance or beach headland to prevent their return.

Most important is the application of the sonic approach to the protection of the survivors of tragedies at sea. Survivors could be protected by means of small, compact transmitting units which, when activated and suspended below the swimmer, would transmit a signal barrier in all directions. Commercial and military aircraft would be equipped with fully automatic sonic repellents which, in the event of a ditching at sea, would be activated on contact with the water and establish a sound barrier to safeguard survivors against shark attack. These units, which have already been designed in part, will be mounted into the fuselage of the plane and if a ditching occurs will activate on hydrostatic (water) pressure, to be jetted down beneath and then sideways to clear the hull. The units will be buoy marked, and will not only establish a sonic shark repellent barrier, but will transmit over a limited radius a distress call for searching boats and planes. The buoy markers will also be fitted with a flashing red light to mark their position during the hours of darkness. Into one of the units would be incorporated the aircraft's "black box" containing the data of the plane's flight performance prior to the crash. Shipping would be protected in a like manner, with units that could be cast into the waters surrounding the disaster site.

During my years of research aimed at perfecting the positive all-purpose shark repellent I have often been asked if the effort is really worth it when one considers the chances of being taken by a shark. As one of my friends once told me, "The only time a shark will be able to get me, is if it can fit up through my bath plug-hole!" In coastal waters the chances of a shark attack can be compared to the chances of being struck by lightning. But there is the ever-present fear of shark attack, and this fear robs us of many of our best inshore waterways as areas for relaxation and enjoyment.

At sea the danger of being mauled by a shark is ever present. Anyone who falls overboard from a boat in the ocean is likely to fall into the jaws of a shark and suffer a shocking death. It is in the open ocean that the appalling loss of human life has occurred, that the horrifying massacre of helpless swimmers has been witnessed by those who have been fortunate enough to survive. One only has to read of the American vessel that was torpedoed amidships some hundred miles off the South American coast. The ship went to the bottom and dozens of survivors took to the boats and rafts. A seaman named Izzy survived eighty-three days on a raft, and he told of the terror of drifting in shark-infested waters.

> You could hear guys hollering for help as the ship went down, screaming that sharks were attacking them and there was nothing you could do, and then maybe they would stop screaming and you wouldn't hear them after that or maybe a guy would stop screaming right in the middle of a yell and you would know that something certainly got him.

I tell my critics, "To have witnessed the horror of a shark attack is sufficient to keep me at my task until success is achieved." Being eaten alive is not a pleasant way to die.

My early experimental work with underwater sound transmission was greatly hampered by the lack of suitable equipment. Nothing for this purpose was manufactured, and I was forced virtually to design and construct my own. This often proved very costly and sometimes inadequate for the task, but I carried on. I was at that time restricted to low-voltage equipment, since my power source comprised a number of 12-volt heavy-duty batteries. These were heavy and awkward, and required repeated charging after each extended period of use.

The surface equipment I was using was reasonably easy to come by, particularly from disposal stores, and consisted of tape recorder, amplifier and, later, an audio signal generator, all of which were battery powered. To obtain a transducer, I had to waterproof a loudspeaker, and this presented many unexpected problems: none of these was ever really satisfactory. Often work would come to an abrupt halt as water seeped into the transducer and shorted the unit. Then would commence the frustrating and often hopeless task of drying out the loudspeaker. Sometimes the voice coil would be useless and beyond repair. Various methods of waterproofing the loudspeakers were experimented with, and these included using heavy plastic and rubber bags, metal containers, sealed wooden or plexiglass boxes, and a host of other improvisations, some of which had to be abandoned immediately because the resulting signal distortion made the container useless. The best results were achieved with specially modified household pressure cookers, which increased my effective operational depth to fifty feet or more, although I managed to flood one unit at seventy-five feet when I became too venturesome.

My method of transmitting sounds under water was simple and effective. In my boat would be the tape recorder, which played its signals into the amplifier; both were battery powered. Attached to the amplifier was the cable outlet of my specially waterproofed loudspeaker (transducer), perhaps twenty or thirty feet below on the sea-floor. I had only to set the tape in motion and then enter the water with my diving equipment to observe the results of the experiment. When I first started this work I was using blood and offal as a means of attracting sharks to the vicinity of the tests. I soon found that recording the underwater noises of someone splashing or thrashing about in the water, then replaying this distress stimulus on the tape recorder, was a much more effective method of attracting sharks. I later modified and improved on this technique by recording the noises of speared fish, which proved to be a most successful means of summoning sharks. This achievement was not without its cost. I flooded and ruined every microphone I possessed; and it was not until I was able to obtain, through devious methods, the much sought-after hydrophone that I finally overcame the problem of calling in sharks to the test site.

The start of my test tapes would then comprise the recorded distress signals for a number of minutes, after which the repellent sounds under evaluation would be transmitted. Later I was to improve on this method of sound delivery. Through the use of a second tape recorder I could deliver distress stimulus continuously while employing the second tape to transmit the repellent signals under investigation. This meant the use of a further amplifier and waterproofed loudspeaker and placed a serious strain on my already limited power supplies.

I started the research project by recording a variety of sounds. These were many and varied, and included gun shots and explosions, human voices, screams, babies crying, school children yelling and cheering, dogs barking, lions roaring, bells, gongs, whistles, sirens, musical instruments; mechanical sounds such as a circular saw cutting wood, jack-hammers, the thumping of steel plates, auto crashes, express trains, jet and piston engines, and a host of other everyday noises. I also recorded every type of music I could, and this included waltzes, all types of classical music including some opera (which I reasoned could scare anything off, so terrible were the singers), as well as rock-and-roll and the modern "pop" tunes.

It was a strange and wonderful experience to be under water and hear the screaming tyres of a crashing car, gun shots, women yelling and screaming, fire engines and police sirens roaring through the corals: while the fish swam unconcernedly about their business. I soon found that sudden loud noises could have the initial effect of repelling sharks and sending many hurrying from the transmission area. But, with the continued use of the same sounds in the same locality, the sharks soon became accustomed to these noises and ceased to respond or be repelled. I was greatly disappointed when I realized what was happening, for I had not considered the possibility of sharks becoming conditioned to accept these unusual noises.

It must have been bewildering for other divers who happened to be in the vicinity of my early experiments. When I encountered another diving party in my test area, I got much pleasure from observing the effects on them of the various underwater sounds. On one occasion two divers working some distance from my transmission site thought they were suffering from raptures of the deep when they heard the distant sound of an express train thundering over a bridge.

Another time a diver surfaced excitedly and called to his friend in a boat, "Jack, Jack, it sounds like a woman is being murdered down there. I can hear screams and gun shots."

"Ah, rats, mate," came the reply from his companion in the boat. "If you laid off the grog you wouldn't hear a thing." To satisfy himself, the man in the boat then donned a facemask and stuck his head into the water—to be greeted by complete silence, for I had discontinued transmission. There followed a series of exasperated grunts and disgusted sighs while the diver in the water vehemently supported his claims.

Some forms of music, in particular that with an even rhythm such as a classical waltz, seemed to affect varying forms of fish life. Sometimes the fish would respond by becoming quiescent, lolling about in the water close to the transmission source and quietly rocking back and forth, sometimes they would circle the transducer, completely oblivious to my presence, in pairs or alone, and would continue to move round and round until the throbbing pulse of the music stopped. I never tired of playing this form of music under water. It was as though all the animals were lulled into a sense of togetherness while the pulsing beat rolled out across the coral gardens and into the deeper waters beyond.

As soon as I established my charter boat service on Magnetic Island to support the research programme, I extended my field of operations to the Great Barrier Reef. These were exciting days, when I would leave the island far behind in the pre-dawn darkness, speeding along at thirty knots or so over the smooth, moonlit, tropical seas. I was filled with the spirit of adventure, seeking new and wonderful horizons, an explorer in my own right. Even navigation proved to be an adventure, for although I had the latest in charts, these proved to be often sadly inaccurate. I remember once I was roaring along at thirty knots, perfectly at ease, for the weather was glorious and the seas were calm and mirror-smooth, and I had several hundred feet of water beneath my keel. Suddenly my boat pitched wildly and I was flung on the deck as, with a shuddering halt, I ground up onto a reef. My first impulse was to reach for the two-way radio and call frantically for help, for I was a good sixty miles from the nearest land and alone. But I calmed myself and ventured a look over the side. To my amazement I found I was perched almost high and dry on a reef flat—what reef I did not know, for its presence was unmarked on the chart. Where I was there was over two hundred feet of water, or so my chart said. The glassy smooth surface of the water, reflecting the blue sky, had hidden the reef from my sight; otherwise I'd have seen the differing colours of the water and known what they meant, for the reef was covered with only a few inches of water, having been almost exposed by the falling tide. I quickly lowered myself over the side and inspected the hull. Here I had been fortunate indeed, for the top of the reef was a weathered flat expanse of limestone, here and there dotted with a stunted growth of coral. These growths I had missed as I crashed onto the reef and slithered along on the keel. The only damage appeared to be scratches in the fibreglass along the bottom, and none of these were deep enough to cause concern. But it was the motors that worried me most, for these had struck the reef with a sickening jar, to be flung upwards and then dragged along the reef face. I was relieved to find the propellers intact, and the only apparent damage was a small dent in the metal of the steering rudder below each propeller. The motors had run wildly for a few seconds when they were flung out of the water, and had been screaming insanely until I had reached the throttles and slammed these to the stop position. I waited anxiously for the rising tide to float me free from the reef top to deeper water where I could start the motors and determine the damage. My boat was a 20-foot fibreglass cabin cruiser equipped with two powerful outboard motors. She had a double hull and was a sound seaworthy vessel equipped with the latest navigation aids, including a depth sounder. This I could not use when under full power, for the speed of the hull through the water was such that the returning echo of the depth sounder did not reach the surface until I had long since passed. I also had two-way radio and other safety devices.

At last the rising tide lifted the boat and she drifted free of the reef. It was with trembling hand that I turned the starter—to be rewarded with an instant roar of power. "At least I have one motor to take me home," I thought as I checked its performance. The second motor also instantly sprang to life, and both ran sweetly together as I moved away from the reef and out into open water. But I had learnt my lesson. Never again did I travel at high speed in unknown waters. Local knowledge is of far greater value than all the charts in the world.

Gradually I was able to extend my research activities to cover a distance of almost 120 miles of the Reef, ranging from the Dunk Island reefs of Beaver and Taylor, in the north, to Mid Reef, which is well south of Townsville. Sometimes I would spend several days at sea, anchoring behind a sheltering reef during the night, but always keeping an eye on the weather and monitoring the daily forecasts. Sometimes these didn't hold true, and I remember once, after spending the night behind Mid Reef, I woke and listened to the first forecast of the day. This was for a continuation of fine, calm weather with light variable winds up to five knots. Certainly the weather at the time was perfect, with not a breath of wind to ruffle the glassy-smooth surface of the sea. I busied myself in preparation for the day's research and chanced to look up at the distant horizon towards the south. I was surprised to see this had suddenly taken on the appearance of corrugated iron, and watched fascinated until I heard the approaching roar of wind. Everything was dropped and I hurriedly freed the anchor and got under way, but not before the first gusts had whipped the surface of the water into angry white-caps. I was fortunate that the wind was from the south, for by applying full power to the motors I was able to move ahead of the wind within a minute or two. Homeward bound, I sped along at thirty knots once again in calm unmoved waters, but closely followed by the advancing storm. On reaching Magnetic Island, I barely had time to secure my boat to its moorings before a strong southerly wind of between 25 and 30 knots arrived.

As soon as I realized that there was to be no short cut to success, I had to reconsider the programme. A new approach was adopted. This was to use pure signal tones over a wide frequency range, one of the objects being to try to establish the perception or reception limits of a shark. To perfect the sonic approach to shark repellents I ought first to determine the exact limits of perception of each species of shark under investigation. This I could not do. Funds were not available to buy the sophisticated laboratory equipment and other facilities that would be needed for a project of this magnitude. But I still hoped to be able to establish some approximate indication of the shark's perception through my field research.

I knew that the low frequencies, including the infrasonic tones that are below the human threshold of hearing, could attract or call-in sharks to any given locality if the signal was presented in a "pulsed" fashion. Perhaps then, I reasoned, the ultrasonic frequencies could be employed to repel sharks. The average human is capable of hearing sounds up to about 16,000 cycles per second; or, to use the new international radio terminology, hertz per second (being so called after the discoverer). I have a perception limit well above average despite a long diving career that can be injurious to hearing ability, and I can detect sounds as high as 17,500 cycles per second (c.p.s.). My equipment was capable of transmitting in excess of 30,000 c.p.s.; and to ensure that it was functioning correctly I had to enlist the services of a friendly dog. I would set up my transmitting gear in a quiet room and put the dog in one corner; then I would begin to transmit sounds in the ultrasonic frequency range. By observing the dog's behaviour I was able to establish whether the signals were being received, for usually its ears would prick up immediately and it would look inquiringly at the signal source. Some dogs are capable of hearing sounds as high as 45,000 c.p.s., and dogs were at that time my only means of checking my equipment. I had not the funds to buy the necessary test units.

To generate the pure signal tones required for the next phase of my research undertaking, I bought an audio signal generator. This unit was capable of delivering three separate types of sound waves. These were: sine waves, which when viewed on an oscillograph had an even fluctuating pattern like that of a steeply waving line; square waves, where the pattern as implied by the name was flattened and squared at the top and bottom of the wave; and lastly complex waves, which consisted of a combination of both sine and square waves.

Ultrasonics didn't work. The sharks completely ignored these signals, and it was soon obvious that they were not receptive to such high sounds. I was bitterly disappointed. The entire series of tests had yielded nothing, and I felt that I had wasted my time and money. The only positive reaction had been when a school of dolphins arrived on the scene and had swum excitedly about the transducer. I had been transmitting short intervals of varying high-frequency sounds, and it appeared that these had attracted the dolphins. They stayed for a while, and then each of the graceful animals swam over to where I was observing the experiment, my presence being no doubt betrayed to these highly intelligent creatures by the continuous stream of air bubbles that issued from my diving equipment. They swam past so close I could have touched each one as it enthusiastically turned and twisted in acknowledgment. I called a greeting, then they were gone, and I experienced a feeling of loneliness and longing as I watched them disappear into the surrounding gloom. Perhaps one day man will be able to communicate with these wonderful animals and learn additional secrets of the sea. I have been told that in Russia to kill a dolphin or a porpoise is to risk capital punishment.

Of course it was impossible for me to determine that sharks in general were not receptive to ultrasonics. Until such time as *all* the known species had been experimented with, such a statement could not be made with any degree of accuracy. During my experimental work I was dealing only with a few of the hundreds of species of shark that inhabited the oceans.

It was not until many years later, in fact during February 1972, that I was to have second thoughts on the subject of ultrasonics. Professor Albert L. Tester, the senior Professor of Zoology at the University of Hawaii, was visiting my research headquarters on Magnetic Island, where I had been based for some time while engaged on Crown of Thorns starfish research. Al was visiting the island to discuss the sonic approach to shark repellents and our possible involvement in a joint expedition during 1973. The Janss Foundation of America had offered Professor Tester the use of their fully equipped scientific research vessel, R.V. *Searcher*, during 1973, to promote scientific research in the Pacific. This would be a wonderful opportunity for us to experiment with the sonic approach and the pelagic species of shark, for the vessel was fitted with closed-circuit underwater television. Little experimental work had been undertaken with the pelagic sharks, because of the danger to research personnel.

During our discussions, I happened to mention to Al one of the few encounters I had had with the pelagic species during my research, in this instance the much-feared White Shark. I had been transmitting sound waves which fluctuated from the sonic (audible) to the ultrasonic. A number of these modulating signal patterns were superimposed one upon the other on a specially prepared tape. During following tests a White Shark had responded to the signals by appearing to lose all control over its movements, and had literally gone mad. It had attempted to bite its own tail, twisting about in the most impossible positions, and appeared to turn itself almost inside out. Following this, the shark exploded from the water—it leapt completely above the surface, to land back with a resounding splash before making off at a great speed never to return.

Al then told me of a similar experience he had had while experimenting with a shark in a land-based tank. He was transmitting a strong signal of ultrasonic sound waves and the shark had responded and behaved in the same manner as my test animal. The shark, of course, could not escape from the signals, and finally reached what appeared to be a state of complete mental and physical exhaustion. During Al's experiment the signal source had been strong; so strong, in fact, that when the investigators placed their hands in the tank water they could feel the ultrasonic vibrations.

It is not beyond the realms of possibility that sound vibrations could prove so intolerable to a shark that a total mental collapse could result, perhaps even death. This is not as fantastic as it may seem. A shark has a massive system (the lateralis system) whereby it receives sound vibrations; and perhaps this could be "saturated", with the nervous system and brain becoming overloaded, resulting in a classic example of nervous breakdown, or even death. But such a signal pattern, if ever perfected, would not be employed to repel sharks. I feel that it is essential that the repellent signal used should merely repel, and not kill or injure the animals. The matter does warrant further detailed experimental work, however; for through sound we may be able to develop the ultimate weapon to kill sharks when and where this becomes necessary.

Even the fish ignored the ultrasonics and continued on their way completely unconcerned. The only amusement I could find was to vibrate open certain shell fish; but this was little consolation in the gloom of failure that enveloped me.

During this period of research with ultrasonics and while working the outer Barrier Reef complex called the Great Sand Cay north of Townsville, now also known as the Derham Sand Cay, I became so disgusted with the project that I reverted to my tapes containing the variety of recorded noises first experimented with. I was on the outer ocean side of a reef at a depth of thirty feet, where the steep decline of the coral tumbled down to a considerable depth below. I received a jolt when a White Shark put in an appearance and began to move back and forth through the water close to the transducer. Although the shark was only about eight feet in length, I was extremely apprehensive as it eyed me off, no doubt as a possible meal. My hand was ready to ring the buzzer that would have warned my surface assistant to discontinue the signals; but I waited while the tape delivered its assorted jumble of audible noises. None of these appeared to affect the shark, for it continued its patrol, moving slowly back and forth. Then the music commenced, but still with no visual effect until almost the end of the tape, where I had recorded one of the Beatles' popular numbers, "Oh Yeah". As soon as the first jangling bars of this hit tune echoed out through the water the White Shark became extremely agitated and commenced a series of fast, short manoeuvres. When the Beatles themselves started bellowing their song, the shark exploded in a frenzy of activity and made off at an incredible speed. It was obvious that the animal was not a Beatles fan, for it did not return, despite my attempts to lure it back with attractive distress stimulus signals.

My activities were then altered to include the pure signal tones at the sonic or audible sound level. Here at last I started to have some measure of success, for certain frequencies appeared to have a definite effect on some species of shark.

Although Magnetic Island had an abundance of sharks, mainly Tigers, Hammerheads and Whalers, as well as the numerous small reef varieties, I found that out on the Great Barrier Reef they were more prolific. My research animals in Magnetic Island waters were soon to be drastically depleted, for the Government introduced shark meshing to protect the swimmers that flocked to the area. So I was forced to move farther afield, and even worked the outer patch reefs of the Great Barrier, which I found particularly rewarding with the number of sharks that presented themselves during the experimental programme. Here the water was generally crystal clear, and good protection was afforded to me by the large overhanging coral growths. I was able to conceal myself beneath a coral overhang and watch the sharks in comparative safety: as the only avenue of attack was a frontal one, and this at times was greatly restricted by the surrounding growths. I was armed with a hand spear to which was attached an explosive head, powered by a 12-gauge shotgun cartridge, and it gave me a measure of comfort if a curious shark approached my hiding-place.

The research had become extremely complex and difficult, for I soon found that no one pure signal tone would yield the repellent effect I was seeking. It was obvious that I would have to combine a number of pure signal tones in the one transmission pattern. In one sense it appeared that the work had been simplified to some degree because the dangerous sharks I was experimenting with were not receptive to sounds above about 7,000 c.p.s. But the difficulties were compounded when I found that, while all sharks responded to the same basic low or infrasonic frequencies employed to attract or guide them in to their prey, this did not apply where a repellent signal was concerned. There was a considerable variation between species as to the effectiveness of the repellent sounds: I found that the signal that would repel the Tiger Shark was not effective for the Whaler Sharks. The Hammerhead species responded to an entirely different combination of pure tones. And when I attempted to combine the repellent frequencies of the Tiger and Whaler Sharks, the resulting signal distortion rendered both patterns virtually useless.

By the end of two years' research involving pure tones some progress had been made. Already, through the application of these sounds, I had been able to achieve a limited repellent effect with the underwater transmission of certain signal patterns. I also began to notice that some species of bony fish were responding to the low-frequency pulse sounds and could be attracted together with the sharks. This mainly involved the larger predatory fish, but the matter warranted further detailed investigation. Moray eels would also be attracted by the distress stimulus and would gather round the transducer pecking away at the waterproof housing in an effort to reach the source of the attractive signals.

I found that I had to be very careful when transmitting the distress stimulus: twice sharks had become excited and seized the underwater loudspeaker in their jaws, and once the unit was completely wrecked when water flooded in. By employing the continuous transmission of the distress signals I was better able to evaluate the repellent effect of the tones under investigation, the object of the experiment being to repel the shark from the source of the attractive stimulus. To avoid the sharks' becoming conditioned to the signals and then ignoring them, I continually varied my test location, and moved from reef to reef.

To ensure that the experimental data were being accurately recorded I had special forms printed. These greatly simplified the recording process and made provision for such information as the water temperature and depth and clarity, the prevailing conditions, the species encountered (with number, time, date and exact location), as well as numerous other facts relevant to the programme.

While I was working on the Great Barrier Reef reports filtered down from Green Island, where it was said that the Crown of Thorns starfish were destroying the coral. I had seen little evidence of these starfish before I left the Reef in September 1965. In fact, only six specimens were sighted during a period of five years' research, and this involved an area of approximately 120 miles of reef. On two occasions, while transmitting sound under water, I had seen a Crown of Thorns in the close vicinity of the transducer curl into a ball and fall from the coral onto the sea floor. This was reported on my data forms, but I placed little importance on the matter as at that time I did not realize the magnitude of the threat posed to the Great Barrier Reef.

By mid-1965 I had been moderately successful and was able to repel three species of known or reputed man-eating sharks (the Whaler, Tiger and Hammerhead), and a further two species (the Bronze Whaler and Grey Nurse) were responding favourably.

A number of problems were now presenting themselves. I had so neglected my charter boat business, owing to my research involvement, that this was far from a financial success. Debts were mounting, and I was unable to replace urgently needed research equipment. In addition, I had reached the stage at which I needed to evaluate my experimental results in an entirely new geographic location. I wanted to be sure that the signals I was having success with in North Queensland waters would yield the same positive results elsewhere.

I had had many reports from New Guinea on the large number of dangerous sharks there, with details of attacks on humans. This, I thought, would be the ideal place to further the experimental programme; and so I made plans.

In September 1965 I left Magnetic Island and, heavily in debt, flew to Port Moresby to take a job with a well-established firm. This was to prove the wisest move I ever made, and to ensure a continuation of the research undertaking.

6

New Guinea was to prove particularly lucrative for me, and I quickly got out of the red. I was controlling a newly established security organization for one of the biggest concerns in the Territory. With a number of skilled divers, I formed a small and profitable diving enterprise. The wages paid to natives at that time averaged around $A7.00 a week and I could employ a top diver for that amount. By increasing my boys' weekly wage to $20.00 a week and in some cases more, I soon had a reliable, loyal and well-disciplined team. All my profits were immediately channelled into my research project, and I lived for the week-ends and holidays when I could once again devote my time to it.

The sharks in New Guinea waters were particularly large and aggressive, although the species encountered were basically the same as those found on the Great Barrier Reef. Even in areas such as the back reaches of Port Moresby Harbour, including the upper tidal estuaries well past Napa Napa, I was catching sharks between 12 and 14 feet in length. This work was usually carried out at night because of my tight work schedule, the heavy set lines being cleared each evening and then re-baited for the following day. I often made good catches, and one night after a particularly rewarding evening's work, with a number of large sharks on board, I witnessed an incident for which, to this day, I cannot find a satisfactory explanation.

While I was manoeuvring the last of the heavy set lines alongside the launch to remove the captured shark, which was wildly thrashing about in the water, one of my native boys, called Emu, overbalanced and toppled over the side into the darkness. There was an ear-splitting yell and Emu was back on board, bone dry apart from legs wet to his knees, the wetness being clearly visible on his long khaki trousers. How he managed this acrobatic feat will always remain a mystery, for Emu was facing outwards over the rail when he lost balance and disappeared from sight. The next instant he executed his spectacular return and came flying over the rails to land on board facing inwards. Not even poor old Emu could enlighten us. A possible explanation is that Emu landed on the shark's back and got such a fright that he was airbone again in an instant, and had the good fortune to land back on the boat.

Shark attacks took a heavy toll of human life in New Guinea waters while I was in the Territory. No one really knows the number of natives that meet this terrifying fate each year. There is little communication with outlying areas, and some native villages in remote coastal regions rarely see a white man; so that many shark attacks are unrecorded. I investigated a number of the reported attacks, but it was extremely difficult to get the facts from isolated villages.

The late Sir Victor Coppleson first advanced the theory that a shark, having once tasted human blood, might seek out humans and continue to prey on them. Such a shark could be classed as either a local rogue, one having particular territorial rights, or a cruising rogue shark, one that followed a set patrol area of perhaps 60 sea miles or more.

A general pattern of attack has been observed with the Whaler Shark, the species responsible for the majority of attacks in our coastal regions, particularly in tidal rivers and estuaries throughout Australia and New Guinea. The attacking shark strikes its victim only once, and then apparently breaks off the encounter. Various theories have been advanced to explain this behaviour, and the most probable is that the composition of human blood, being unlike anything the shark has experienced before, makes the animal extremely cautious. I remember that Norman Keene, who came to my assistance after the attack on Ken, had told me how he was about to jump from his dinghy near the shore in blood-stained water when suddenly a large shark rushed beneath his boat. He then beached the dinghy before leaping ashore. It was obvious that the attacking shark had remained in the vicinity but did not attempt to strike Ken again. And I was left unmolested as I swam to Ken's rescue and carried him ashore.

Many attacks occur in murky water where the attacking shark cannot see its intended prey and is responding to the attractive sound vibrations echoing outwards through the water from the activities of some clumsy swimmer or child playing. These signals are so similar in pattern to the distress signals emitted by a wounded or sick fish that the attacking shark is only responding to its basic instinctive feeding habits. This no doubt is the factor that has led many a cautious shark to attack a human, and this might not have occurred if the animal had been able to see its prey. In the attack I survived at Woodman's Point, it is likely that the splashing of the two divers who left the water immediately before called the shark back into the area. It was dark when this attack took place, and there could have been no visual contact until the very last moment, when the shark, having isolated me as the source of the attractive stimulus, proceeded to attack.

There are exceptions to this general pattern of behaviour—as there always are exceptions with sharks. The attacking shark has been known to return to its human victim and resume the attack, and a rescuer has sometimes been mauled; but this pattern is comparatively rare with the Whaler Shark. Occasionally, perhaps, a shark that is old or injured, and cannot capture the fish on which it would normally feed, takes a swimmer. Finding that this form of prey can be obtained with a minimum of effort, the shark may then completely alter its normal feeding pattern and continue to attack humans whenever the opportunity presents itself—like the man-eating tiger of India. This may explain how an area that has been free of attack for years suddenly becomes the scene of a series of attacks on swimmers. Dr Coppleson documented a number of such shark-attack sequences in Australian and New Guinea waters, where all available evidence indicated that one shark was responsible.

I was able to confirm this theory after investigating a number of shark attacks in the Rabaul–Duke of York Islands–Southern New Ireland region. The series commenced at about 1 p.m. on 21st August 1966 when two native girls from the Butliwan Village on the Duke of York Islands off Rabaul were attacked and killed by a shark. One of the girls, a seven-year-old, was carried off while her companion, a thirteen-year-old, lost one leg and had the other completely stripped of flesh. She died almost immediately. Shortly afterwards, a large black-coloured shark, estimated to be around 12 feet in length, was sighted. This shark continued to appear in the waters off Butliwan for several weeks, and all attempts by the natives to capture it proved unsuccessful. This area had been free of shark attacks for as long as the villagers could remember. The shark then disappeared.

On 29th October 1966 an eight-year-old native girl called Dakel was bitten completely in half while washing herself in the sea at the mission beach on Lambom Island, off the south-west coast of New Ireland. The following day, 30th October, at Lamassa Island, also on the south-west coast of New Ireland and sixteen miles from the previous attack site, another native girl, Rigel Togias, aged thirteen years, was fatally mauled while swimming. A third attack followed shortly afterwards, and a small native female child was carried off by a shark while being held and bathed in her father's arms. The man was untouched by the attacking shark. After each of these attacks, a large black shark, described by the natives as having the girth of a 44-gallon drum and being about 12 feet in length, was seen cruising off shore over the next two months. This area had been free from attacks for many years, and after the second series of attacks native girls and women were too terrified to enter the sea. There were no further disasters until mid-day on 1st March 1967, when a fourteen-year-old native boy of the Raluana Village was attacked at Barawin Beach on the mainland close to Rabaul. The boy survived the leg injuries inflicted. It was not until 1st September in the same year that the shark again struck, and on this occasion Tony Kamage, twenty-three years old, of Finschhafen, was fatally mauled while spearfishing off Lamassa Island, the scene of the fatal attack on 30th October 1966. All of these recorded attacks took place in an area of roughly sixty sea miles where there had been no attacks for many years.

It appeared likely that the entire series of incidents was the work of one cruising rogue shark. It patrolled the area from the Duke of York Islands along the south-west coast of New Ireland. Other natives may have been taken by this shark in attacks not recorded through lack of communication. The shark had first concentrated on females, perhaps responding to their particular olfactory stimulus. When the native women and girls became too terrified to enter the water, the shark then attacked boys and men. Seven attacks were recorded in just over a year, and in each case the description of the attacking shark was the same. The long intervals between attacks in the latter part of the series indicates the fear that this animal caused the natives; for neither man nor woman nor child would enter the sea for weeks and often months after an attack. If the news was slow in spreading, the shark could strike again in some other isolated area. When I left New Guinea it was not possible for me to remain in contact with this area; but it is likely that the attacks continued until the shark was captured and killed, or was injured during one of its attacks.

My research was at first restricted to the area surrounding Port Moresby, including the numerous small islands of which Fisherman's was the largest. I often spent the weekend on Fisherman's Island hunting for sharks, accompanied by Bruce Poynter who at that time was completing his schooling at Port Moresby High School, and Adriaan de Wit, of the marine base at Napa Napa, and several of our native boys.

Native men in Papua and New Guinea, regardless of age, are called "boys" by Europeans, and I could never get used to calling a middle-aged or an old man "boy". Most of the natives I met were born on either Christmas Day or Good Friday, or so I was informed. There was little recording of births in the numerous native villages, and a man could live and die without his name having ever been recorded by pen on paper. I always found it amusing when a hefty native man with a flourishing beard came to me seeking work, and to my inquiry, "How old are you?" would reply, "Twelve next birthday." Or a small native boy who was about twelve would solemnly inform me that he was forty-five years old.

I found the Papuans and New Guineans likeable and happy people, normally carefree and gay. Only in the large towns were they sometimes objectionable, no doubt through the white man's influence. Natives and alcohol don't go well together; they never have and they never will. It was depressing to see some of these fine people being degraded by excessive drinking. I had made many friends amongst the indigenous people of the Territory and had come to know and respect them.

Most of my native staff were loyal to the point of turning against their own people should the need arise. One day one of my boss native boys came to me and whispered in my ear, "You don't want to trust those niggers, Taubada. They are bad men", as he strove to convince me I should not employ a group of natives from a different tribe. A happy race, they loved playing practical jokes on one another—and, if I was not careful, on me, too.

Shortly after my arrival in Port Moresby I decided to explore the Ianopa River, where fresh-water sharks were said to be found. The river was some distance from Port Moresby, and had to be approached through the jungle or from the coast. I decided to go through the jungle and, rather than walk, I had an old cane armchair mounted onto two carrying poles of stout wood, and sat in it like a jungle lord being borne aloft by four of my native workers. With a jungle helmet and a switching branch of leaves to keep the mosquitoes at bay, I was carried through the forest to the happy chanting of the bearers. This was doing things in grand style, as, I imagined, a Stanley or a Livingstone might have done. But when we approached the river that was our destination, and my boys were wading laboriously through an evil-smelling swamp, one of them stumbled and I was suddenly tipped from my jungle chair and fell face first into the stinking mess. There was a stunned silence as the natives looked at one another and I fought to extract myself from the sucking mass of black mud. As I stood erect there was a hysterical outburst of laughter: I must have looked a sight indeed, being covered from head to foot in shiny black mud with only my eyes glinting white. I decided to walk the rest of the way to the river, and left my jungle chariot where it had fallen. Together with my boys I staggered through the swamp to their accompanying fits of delighted laughter.

On arriving at the river bank I found the water was cool and inviting. I asked my head boy, Umie, if it was safe for me to swim. I was assured vigorously by one and all that it was, and so plunged in to wash away the foul smelling mud from my body and clothes. The water was wonderfully refreshing, and I asked my native friends why they too did not enjoy the water. "No, no, Taubada, too many poop poops," came the reply. I was greatly alarmed, thinking that they were referring to a sewage outlet somewhere up stream, and I hastily scrambled from the water. "What are poop poops?" I demanded of Umie, fearing the worst. Through various signs and spoken words, I was soon aware that poop poops were fresh-water crocodiles. But I had no need to worry: the crocodiles did not attack white men because of their smell, which was offensive to these sensitive creatures. This did nothing to relieve my peace of mind, and I quickly abandoned my plans to dive and explore the waters of the river for evidence of fresh-water sharks. Sharks were one thing, but I drew the line at crocodiles.

While diving at Middle Arm on one of the tidal estuaries of Darwin Harbour, I had good cause to count my lucky stars. I was there as the police diver in search of stolen goods thought to have been dumped in this isolated area.

A few nights before, during a party at Mendle Beach close to Darwin, which had lasted well into the night, the girls decided that they wished to swim. Fortunately before entering the water we drove our cars up over the rise of the beach so that the head-lights shone down into the water: for there on the wet sand at the water's edge was a huge salt-water crocodile, a massive armour-plated creature at least 18 feet in length, and so huge did the beast appear that it looked for all the world like some prehistoric monster in the dim light.

To look for the stolen goods I had to search with my hands through several feet of the soft mud of the sea floor, about 20 feet under water below the old jetty. So murky was the water that I could see nothing, not even my hand when this was placed against the glass of my mask. When I had completed my task and was staggering with my heavy diving equipment through the thick tidal mud towards the shore, I came across the fresh tracks of a large crocodile. These led down to the water to almost the very spot where I had been diving. I had escaped the terrible fate of being seized alive by one of these horrible animals, to be carried away and buried in the mud where I could be devoured at its leisure. I feared these amphibious reptiles far more than any shark, because of their ability to reason and use their animal cunning when tracking down their prey. They were not like the sharks that followed an instinctive pattern of behaviour conditioned by aeons of evolution.

I was soon able to extend my field of operations by using light aircraft to take me and my equipment about the Territory. New Guinea's rugged terrain makes flying hazardous at the best of times, and often heavy clouds suddenly roll in to hide mountain ranges with their jagged peaks. The time I had available for the shark project was restricted not only by my employment but by other research commitments. One of these was an examination of the venomous sea snakes that were prolific in local waters.

On my first dive at Ela Beach, the popular swimming resort of Port Moresby,. I was shocked to see sea snakes swimming in and out amongst the unconcerned and unaware bathers. But it was rarely that these animals became aggressive towards humans: during my research only twice did I excite a sea snake to the point of attack. This was fortunate indeed for me, since I used to approach these venomous snakes within touching distance, and often thrust my camera into their faces to get a good photograph. Specimens were simple to come by and I employed a long bamboo pole with a moving wire loop attached. It was a simple matter to slip the loop over the head of the snake and then tighten the wire, effectively immobilizing the specimen.

Apart from lack of time, my shark research was severely hampered by difficulties with equipment. Not long after my arrival in New Guinea I was to discover that my waterproofed loudspeakers were not giving pure signal tones at varying water depths. The first indication of this problem was a complete reversal of the effect of what had been a successful repellent signal combination against the Whaler Shark. With this signal I had been able to repel these animals during 57 consecutive experiments and felt assured of success. Then came experiment number 58. I attracted three Whaler Sharks into the test area and immediately commenced the transmission of the repellent signal. Two of the sharks responded as anticipated and fled; but the third shark, slightly larger than the others, at first followed suit, then suddenly turned and attacked the transducer, completely wrecking the unit with its powerful jaws. I was stunned. It just didn't seem possible after so much success.

It was with a heavy heart that I realized all my effort was again wasted. But before I was to find the cause of this failure I was to be involved in my second shark attack which, like the first at Woodman's Point, almost cost me my life.

I was working well north of Port Moresby at the extreme end of the outer fringing reef which followed the coast for a considerable distance. Idia Island was a small coral sand cay covered with coarse, stunted scrub, and was inhabited by large lizards and numerous bats or flying-foxes. The water out from the island at the outer edge of the reef was crystal clear, a welcome change from the often turbid waters round much of the New Guinea coastline. I had attracted a number of sharks to the test site, when suddenly I saw a White Shark, around 10 feet or so, move quickly into the area. As well as being alarmed I was greatly surprised, for I had not expected to see this species so far north and so close inshore.

I was well protected from behind by the steeply sloping drop-off of the coral reef face, but this did little to comfort me when I could see that the shark was becoming agitated by the signals. Cursing myself for not doing so before, I reached for the buzzer to alert my surface operator that all sound transmission was to cease. Before I could reach it, the shark turned so quickly that I heard an audible "snap" as its tail flicked around, and it rushed at me from one side. I had time to thrust my explosive-headed hand-spear towards the charging animal, and was rewarded with a shattering bang as the cartridge detonated against the shark's snout. But part of the pole slid between the teeth and jammed in its throat. I clung desperately to the four feet of pole left protruding from the fearsome mouth, but the momentum of the shark's charge carried me sideways through the water at an incredible speed. My facemask was ripped off, one flipper was dislodged, and my aqualung mouthpiece was torn from my mouth.

I let go and fell behind some coral to the sea floor. Struggling for breath, I frantically felt for my mouthpiece and, finding it, slipped it between my lips. I clutched at the spare facemask I always carried attached to my knife belt, fitted it over my head, and quickly cleared it of water by exhaling sharply through my nose. With a desperate feeling of vulnerability I spun around in the water looking for the shark, expecting a second attack at any moment. It had gone and I lost little time in locating my buzzer and signalling for all transmission to stop.

I shot to the surface and vaulted into the waiting boat with such speed that my native assistant jumped from his seat with a startled yell. Apart from numerous cuts and tears in my rubber wet suit and a bad shaking up and bruising (I ached all over for days afterwards), I appeared to be unharmed. But I had had enough. It was suicide to carry on with the aggressive sharks that frequented those waters. I realized, too, that my equipment was just not good enough for the research programme. It would have to be greatly modified and improved before I could hope to carry on with any degree of safety or success.

For the next few months I limited my research to the catching of sharks and studying the biology of the specimens. I simplified my shark-catching technique by setting out the heavy rig, then virtually calling the sharks to the baited hooks with distress stimulus. Once, during these fishing days, I worked a number of sharks into a minor feeding frenzy, and the crazed animals fought each other to get the baited hooks. I landed a fair-sized female Tiger Shark during the resulting commotion and removed the intestines and internal organs. As I threw the disembowelled body back and heaved the insides after it she turned and ate the stuff. As she swallowed her own innards they dropped out of the gigantic slit in her belly.

When in a frenzied state sharks cease to respond to their sensory systems. They become insensible to pain and carry on devouring their kind while they in turn are being devoured alive. The shark I threw back into the water was soon set upon by the others and was quickly reduced to a few pieces of flesh drifting about in the blood-stained water.

76

I asked my import agents in New Guinea, Nigimy, a Dutch firm with offices throughout the world, to try to find me suitable underwater loudspeakers by contacting all the leading electronic equipment manufacturers. The manager of the Port Moresby Office, Berry Janssen, launched himself enthusiastically into the task, and requests for the supply of the equipment were lodged with all the top-name manufacturers. None of the leading electronic people could help, because my specifications were too rigid and too wide. I needed a high-performance underwater transducer capable of transmitting pure signal tones through its entire frequency range regardless of the operational depth, and the maximum depth must be at least 75 feet. The loudspeaker must have a wide frequency response extending from infrasonic to ultrasonic frequencies; it must be compact and easy to handle under water; it must have a high watt output to ensure adequate strength of signal; and the unit must be robust enough to withstand the bite of a shark.

I realized that I could do nothing without such transducers, and the entire project appeared doomed to failure through the lack of suitable equipment. I had been using loudspeakers manufactured by one of Japan's leading electronic equipment specialists, the Pioneer Electronic Corporation of Tokyo. These units I had waterproofed myself. The standard of the equipment was excellent, but it was just not designed for my purpose and was not capable of transmitting pure signal tones at varying water depths with a corresponding variation in pressures. It was obvious that the hydrostatic pressures were affecting the output of the loudspeakers and distorting the signal patterns transmitted. The frequency output at, say, 20 feet under water, varied from the output obtained at 30 feet, and so on. The results of all my previous experimental work were open to suspicion, for I could not determine with any degree of accuracy what the exact repellent frequencies were. I had, of course, an approximate idea of the range; but I did not know to what extent the water pressure had distorted my signal patterns.

These were questions that could be answered only with correctly designed and proven underwater transmitting units. The development costs of such equipment were prohibitive and far more than I could ever hope to earn. Through Berry, I submitted another order to Pioneer in Japan for the supply of underwater loudspeakers with matching high performance amplification units.

I heard nothing for six months. It was as though I had arrived at an insurmountable obstacle—a blank wall on which there were no footholds. The American, Dutch, British, French and Australian electronic equipment manufacturers had all been unable to meet my specifications for the transducers I so urgently needed.

I was in the depths of depression one day, when the phone rang. It was Berry. "How many of those transducers do you want?" he asked. "Pioneer have advised that they are ready for delivery." I was staggered and speechless.

Down at Berry's office, I examined the specification sheets of the new units. They were better than I had dared to hope, with a guaranteed operation depth of up to 100 feet, pure signal tones at all levels, and a frequency response of from 20 to 20,000 c.p.s. at 30 watts output. Constructed of heavy metal and shark-bite proof, the transducers weighed 30 pounds, were 5½ inches in diameter, and only 9½ inches in length. I was overjoyed, and ordered three of the units, each with 150 feet of special underwater cable attached.

I altered my entire equipment layout to units that were mains powered at 240 volts. I bought small portable power generators to meet the electric power requirements. There would be no more handling and carting of heavy batteries, no more extensive delays while these were frequently recharged. I got all new equipment, including high-performance tape recorders, audio signal generators, amplification units, hydrophones, and additional power generators. I had unlimited power at the touch of a starter cord. So now for the first time the research project became independent and I could work wherever I chose.

But I still had to find an alternative research site, for I now considered it too dangerous to attempt any further work in New Guinea waters. While I was waiting for the delivery of my new equipment, I made approaches to a number of foreign Governments. Possible areas of future research were the Philippines, Singapore, the British Solomon Islands, New Caledonia, the Fiji Islands and French Polynesia. I submitted basic research proposals to the appropriate authorities, and received a favourable response from all of them. It was French Polynesia that appeared to offer the best prospects for a continuation of my programme. Although the waters of this region of the Central and South Pacific were prolific in sharks of the known and reputed man-eating species, there was little record of attack. The French Polynesian species appeared to be less aggressive than their Australian and New Guinea counterparts.

I also had a special reason for finally choosing the Central and South Pacific. Here I hoped to find the legendary Great White Shark (*Carcharodon megalodon*), the most terrible monster known to inhabit the seas in ancient times, perhaps 15 million years ago. Though it was thought by most scientists to be extinct, I had reason to suppose that this huge beast still inhabited the deep trenches of the Pacific Ocean. Massive teeth, five inches across the base, have been dredged up from the Central Pacific. These were of recent origin, not fossilized as had been the similar teeth recovered from the Miocene fossil deposits. Marine biologists and naturalists had different opinions about these huge teeth. Some asserted that they were the larger main front teeth of the shark. A shark possessing such teeth would be between 80 and 90 feet in length. Others believed that the teeth were some of the smaller ones from farther back along the jaw. If this were so, then the monster must have been from 110 to 120 feet long!

In Townsville during 1963 the captain of an 85-foot motor vessel told me an interesting story, asking me not to reveal his name because he thought he would be held up to public ridicule. His vessel was en route from Brisbane to Townsville and travelling along the outer edge of the Great Barrier Reef, when something went wrong with the engine. As the weather was calm and the seas smooth, the vessel was heaved to and the repairs commenced. Both the captain and his crew suddenly became aware of a huge shark, moving slowly near their ship. The captain estimated the monster to be as long as, if not longer than, the ship. I asked how he knew it was a shark and not a whale, and he told me that the huge creature had drifted silently beneath his boat.

"It was definitely a shark. I am no damn fool . . . I watched the thing for some minutes, as did my crew, and it had a strange white appearance as it hung there in the water below. Then it drifted away and we never saw it again. My crew also saw the thing, and afterwards we agreed to tell no one, because we knew that we would be branded as fools and liars."

I was convinced that the man was telling the truth; he had

nothing to gain by making up such a story. I knew that the great Australian naturalist, the late David G. Stead, of Sydney, had also recorded another rare occasion when humans caught a brief glimpse of one of these enormous sharks that are related to the present-day White Shark (*Carcharodon carcharias*).

The appearance of this Great White Shark was recorded by Stead in 1918. The monster had caused a sensation among the deepwater cray fishermen at Port Stephens, on the New South Wales coast, where for several days they refused to go to sea to their regular fishing grounds in the vicinity of Broughton Island. David Stead reports:

> The men had been at work on the fishing grounds—which lie in deep water—when an immense shark of almost unbelievable proportions put in an appearance, lifting pot after pot containing many crayfish, and taking, as the men said, "pots, mooring lines and all". These crayfish pots, it should be mentioned, were about 3 feet 6 inches in diameter and frequently contained from two to three dozen good-sized crayfish each weighing several pounds. The men were all unanimous that this shark was something the like of which they had never dreamed of. In company with the local Fisheries Inspector I questioned many of the men very closely and they all agreed as to the gigantic stature of the beast. But the lengths they gave were, on the whole, absurd. I mention them, however, as an indication of the state of mind which this unusual giant had thrown them into. And bear in mind that these were men who were used to the sea and all sorts of weather, and all sorts of sharks as well. One of the crew said the shark was "three hundred feet long at least!" Others said it was as long as the wharf on which we stood—about 115 feet! They affirmed that the water "boiled" over a large space when the fish swam past. They were all familiar with whales, which they had often seen passing at sea, but this was a vast shark. They had seen its terrible head which was "at least as large as the roof of the wharf shed at Nelson's Bay". Impossible, of course! But these were prosaic and rather stolid men, not given to "fish stories" nor even to talking at all about their catches. Further, they knew that the person they were talking to (myself) had heard all the fish stories years before! One of the things that impres-

The author samples 78-year-old rum and stout salvaged from the wreck
of the *Denton Holme*

Apprentice Andy Cassidy removes the brass porthole from metal plate
salvaged from the *Denton Holme*

The new landing barge that sank during the cyclone at Cocos-Keeling Islands (before salvage attempts)

The Picnic Bay Hotel, Magnetic Island, after the cyclone of 24th December 1971

Trainee Robert Chilcott removes the young from a shark captured in
Rangiroa lagoon

Papa (*right*) and Theodore unload the day's catch at the Avatoru fisheries outpost

Divers sink the new shark cage into the maelstrom area of the lagoon

Divers at work in the lagoon preparing for shark experiments

Robert beaches the dinghy in the shallows of the lagoon

Didia and Robert hurry back to the boat after being scolded by Mama for being last on board

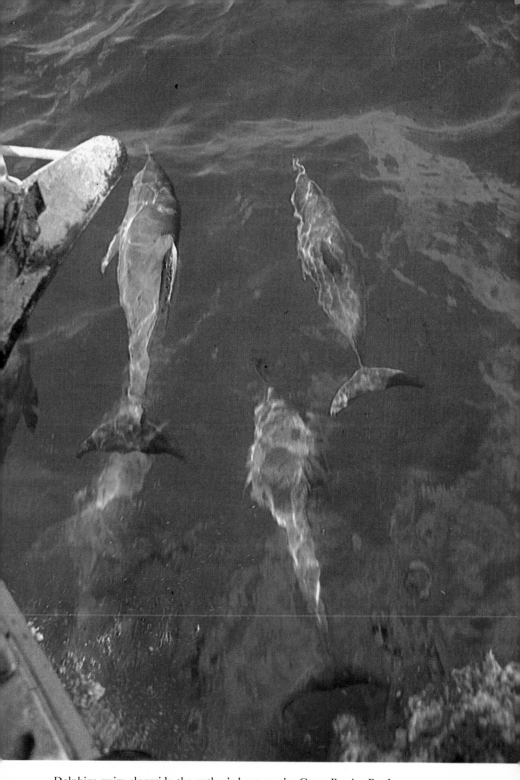
Dolphins swim alongside the author's boat on the Great Barrier Reef

Setting out the shark-catching rig in the lagoon

sed me was that they all agreed as to the ghostly whitish colour of the vast fish. The local Fisheries Inspector of the time, Mr Paton, agreed with me that it must have been something really gigantic to put these experienced men into such a state of fear and panic.

Of particular interest to me was the fact that the Polynesians had recorded the presence of the Great White Shark during their voyages around the Pacific. These monstrous fish had been sighted as they crossed the ocean expanses in their frail canoes. With the aid of the deep-sea transmission of distress stimulus, together with a fish graph camera, I was hoping to be able to record the presence of these huge animals. This research would have to be undertaken in the Central and South Pacific, the region where it appeared the Great White Shark might still inhabit the deep unexplored regions of the ocean. I realized that such huge animals would not be prolific and probably numbered but a few; but perhaps somewhere in the dark unknown depths they could be found and recorded. There was no reason why this huge fish should have become extinct, when its smaller and almost specifically identical relative, the present-day White Shark, still roamed the oceans of the world.

Food would present no problem of survival to this massive shark, for the giant sperm whales dived down thousands of feet into the domain of such deep-sea creatures in search of squid. The giant squid that still exist in the deep ocean regions around the world would supply ample food for such a shark. These huge squids are known to reach an enormous size. A specimen just on 100 feet in length was recently found washed up on a beach of the South Island of New Zealand. When subsequently examined by scientists, it was found to have discs on its tentacles with a diameter of 6 inches, and this was then believed to be the maximum size attained by these creatures. However, a Russian whale chaser later harpooned a large sperm whale. When this was dragged aboard the mother ship for processing it was found to have giant disc marks over much of its body. These were measured, and they were 18 inches in diameter. The monstrous squid with such discs and tentacles must have been in the vicinity of 200 feet in length! It takes little imagination to picture the awesome battle that must have raged in the black bowels of the ocean between this huge whale and the horrible squid, a monster beyond all proportion, so huge that it could bring a whale to a standstill. It is indeed fortunate that such creatures rarely visit the sunlit surface layers of the ocean.

During my travels around the Territory I visited Samarai, on the southernmost tip of Papua, where a delightful string of coral-surrounded islets reach out into the clear sparkling waters of the Coral Sea. It was here that I heard an interesting story. A native from the Solomon Islands told me how at his fishing village the natives had mastered the art of calling in sharks. They also employed a method of attracting sharks to settle love affairs. When there is more than one suitor for a village maiden, it is not uncommon for one of the men involved to eliminate his rival in a novel way. A string of coconut discs, fashioned in a certain way, are threaded onto a cord and then secretly hidden beneath the canoe of the rival. The unsuspecting native paddles his canoe out to the fishing grounds, while all the time the clicking noise of the coconut shells is attracting sharks. Soon, unknown to him, he has a string of hungry followers, and when he enters the water he is promptly attacked and devoured—or so I was informed.

The villagers were said also to attract sharks with the coconut discs threaded onto a circle of bamboo, placing the rattle in the water and shaking it until the sharks would move up to the canoe. When the shark moved alongside a vine rope fashioned into a noose and suspended from a heavy bamboo pole was slipped over its head, and so the animal was captured. The native promised to bring me back such a coconut rattle when next he visited Papua, but I was never to see the man again.

I was sufficiently interested to report the incident to Helen L. Hayes, the then head of the Oceanic Biology Department of the Office of Naval Research in Washington. I told her that, when questioned, the native said the clicking noise of the coconut shells was similar to that made by a crayfish when caught. This noise could indeed attract a shark, for while taking crays myself I have noticed that their struggles attract sharks. Helen Hayes later replied that it would be interesting if I could record the "clicking", then compare the frequencies with those being employed to call in sharks. The Office of Naval Research had no previous knowledge of this native method.

After my return from the 1968 research season in French Polynesia, I was having lunch at the Australian Museum in Sydney with Jack Garrick and Gilbert Whitley (two of Australia's leading authorities on sharks) who had undertaken to check my identifications of the sharks I had recorded in the Central and South Pacific. I casually told the tale of the coconut shells, and Gilbert said, "But of course. We have a set of this apparatus used by the Solomon Island natives downstairs as one of the exhibits."

After lunch we went down to have a look. Sure enough, there they were, just as they had been described by the native years before. The only item missing was the shark lure employed to settle lovers' affairs. Gilbert had never heard of this, but I am now sure that this, too, was a true story.

I have learnt that when dealing with sharks and "shark tales" it is best to doubt nothing, for many strange and often impossible-sounding stories are true, or have a strong element of truth. I have heard many tales of shark worship by the Pacific Islanders, of human sacrifices to the Lord of the Deep, sacrifices made to protect all the villagers from shark attack. And strangely they do seem to be protected, for all the natives, including children, swim unconcerned amongst the sharks and none is molested. There are many other weird stories about sharks, some humorous, some tragic, others too fantastic to comprehend; but whenever I have the opportunity to learn something new about sharks, even if it is a shark tale, I listen and record for future reference. I no longer doubt until I can prove that what was stated was false.

I left Port Moresby in September 1967, after just over two years in the Territory, and flew to Tahiti via Sydney. Negotiations had been completed with the French authorities after several months of correspondence and investigation. The programme had been greatly enlarged to include detailed research into underwater sound transmission and its possible value in the commercial fishing of bony fish and crustaceans. A shark-tagging programme was also included, and it was intended to mark a large number of lagoon and pelagic sharks with numbered identification discs. The initial project was to extend over the 1967-68 period, and I was to work in association with the Institute of Medical Research of French Polynesia, which had its headquarters at Papeete, the capital of Tahiti. My several tons of equipment—which included the latest in underwater sound transmitting and recording gear, motion film equipment (vital to record under water the results of each experiment), diving units, and a host of other items—had already left Port Moresby by steamer as I boarded my flight for French Polynesia.

I felt that at last the die was cast for a successful conclusion of the project, that the sonic method of repelling sharks would soon become a reality.

7

Tahiti was beautiful, its lush tropical vegetation lit with brilliant splashes of colour from the exotic plants and flowers. It rained almost every day, just short sharp showers, and these sent cascading waterfalls and silver rivers winding down from the jagged mountains of the interior. They were soon lost amongst the jungle-covered slopes, to reappear at the water's edge where they tumbled to meet the sea. So inaccessible is the interior of the island that much of it remains untrodden by man to this very day. Coral fringing reefs form a massive circular lagoon, bordered along most of its length by black volcanic sand beaches. Luxuriant tropical growth spreads almost to the lagoon edge, and provides pleasant shade for bathers in the warm clear waters. Children are everywhere, laughing, playing, skipping and running, their almost naked bodies tanned to a deep bronze.

It was just after midnight when my flight arrived at Papeete airport. Here I was ushered through Immigration to Customs, where I anticipated some considerable delay; for I was carrying my concealable firearm and numerous dangerous drugs. I had already obtained approval from the French for the entry of these restricted items, but I had been forewarned about their love of bureaucracy. I was pleasantly surprised when the senior Customs official checked my passport again and said enthusiastically in

English, "Monsieur Brown of the Medical Institute, welcome to Tahiti." There was much discussion in French as I was hurried down the line of Customs officers, my baggage untouched. Although I could not understand the language, I caught occasional words—"Monsieur Brown" . . . "Institut de Recherches Médicales". I shook hands with all those present before being bundled into a waiting car to be driven to the Hotel Matavai.

I was within walking distance of the Medical Institute, and the following morning presented myself at the Director's office. No one appeared to speak or understand English, so I was much relieved to find, on being ushered into his office, that Dr Malarde spoke the language fluently. He was a small and frail-looking man, with a pleasant smile and quiet manner. I instinctively liked Louis Malarde, sensing his goodness and his dedication to humanity. He was enthusiastic about my research project, and we discussed all aspects of the coming programme. I was to have unlimited use of all the facilities of the Institute, and was to work in close co-operation with Dr Raymond Bagnis, the head of the Medical Oceanographic Branch. Before meeting Ray Bagnis I was shown over the Institute by Dr Malarde, this being a two-storey whitewashed building, shaded by the massive spread of several huge trees. At that time the building was undergoing alterations and additions, and we continued our inspection to the methodical blows of several carpenters' hammers.

Dr Raymond Bagnis was seated at his desk surrounded by liquid-filled bottles containing a varying assortment of crabs, lobsters and fish, and from behind his desk the preserved head of a small shark glared at me. Young and athletic-looking and deeply sun-tanned, Dr Bagnis was a former captain in the French Navy who had turned to the field of medicine. We were soon having lunch in the cool comfort of his bungalow, set in a grove of flowering trees at the edge of the lagoon.

Shortly afterwards I called at the Governor's Administration offices to pay my respects and submit, in person, my research proposal to the Government. Being dressed in a dark suit with collar and tie, I was glad to enter the air-conditioned comfort of the imposing structure, and was surprised when the military policemen guarding the entrance sprang to attention and saluted as I passed. As I moved along the corridor furtive glances were thrown in my direction, until, guided by the notices attached to each door, I came to the office of the Secretary-General. The Secretary-General, Monsieur Langlois, did not speak English, and I had no French; so I was taken to the Governor's Bureau D'Etudes and there introduced to Monsieur André Babst, the personal translator to the Governor, Monsieur Sicurani.

Andrew Babst spoke perfect English with a strong American accent, and at first I thought he was an American; but he was very much a Frenchman, and a truer or more loyal one never trod this earth. A former helicopter pilot, much decorated, he had seen active service in Indo-China and the French African possessions. Then he became interested in diving and the underwater world.

I quickly outlined my research proposal and Andrew asked what my requirements were. Since a basic understanding of the French language was essential for my work, I asked permission to attend the Lycée Gauguin, the Papeete High School, for several weeks. I also required approval to work in the Tuamotu Archipelago, a string of coral islands that were renowned shark areas. Many other requests were made: the supply of a suitable small boat to use during the research programme, transportation of equipment to the islands, personnel, accommodation. . . . "Too imposing a list," I thought, as Andrew Babst made notes for his superiors.

I was then taken to meet Lieut.-Colonel Jean Garnier, Andrew's immediate superior, who was to approach the Governor on my behalf. Colonel Garnier was a tall, thin, erect man conditioned by many years of military service to command respect. The authority of his bearing was tempered by a pleasant personality and a winning smile, and he instantly placed me at ease. His English was perfect. He quickly checked my list of requirements and glanced at his watch. "The Governor will be available at two this afternoon. Would it be convenient for you to return then?" I quickly replied that it would and, accompanied by Andrew, took my leave.

"The Colonel is sorry to have to keep you waiting," explained Andy—for he preferred to be called by his first name, and this shortened to "Andy"—"but as it is almost 11.30 the Administration Offices are about to close for lunch, and will not re-open till two this afternoon."

Before we departed Andy drew me to one side and whispered, "Could you do me a favour and not dress as you are on your return? Only the Governor wears a suit in Tahiti, and your presence caused much concern this morning. Many of the staff thought you were a senior official from Paris. Casual dress such as mine is all that is required—slacks and open shirt."

At two sharp I again presented myself at the Colonel's office, to be greeted by a smiling Andy.

"All is approved by the Governor, and you are to start back at school tomorrow morning. The headmaster is expecting you at 7.30 when the classes start."

Andy asked me to visit his home that evening for dinner, and there I had the pleasure of meeting his charming wife, Janene, and his three boys, Nicky, Christoff and Frederick.

Monsieur Leon Depierre, the Headmaster of the Lycée Gauguin, could not speak a word of English, but soon the English Master, Philippe Lenoir, arrived and commenced to translate. I was to start my lessons with the youngest children and was allocated a number of different classes where the age of the pupils ranged from ten to fourteen years. My studies were confined to French grammar and literature, and my teachers, who included André Couraud, Gilbert Pestureau and Guy Denarie, soon became good friends. During my "off-periods" I was allowed to use the staff room where I could continue my studies. At first the children were mystified by this stranger in their midst; but soon I was accepted by even the smallest and youngest, to be enthusiastically greeted each morning by a long line of boys and girls waiting to give me the customary handshake and, as I became better acquainted with some, the polite kiss on each cheek. Many of the children were from France, particularly from Paris, and were in French Polynesia through their parents being posted there. In one of my classes was the Governor's ten-year-old son, and in others the children of senior French Government officials. At an official function to which a number of overseas diplomats were invited, my host informed a senior visiting American, "This is Monsieur Theo Brown who attends high school with my twelve-year-old son." There was a strange silence while those present digested this piece of information.

Those were happy days while I strove to master the language. My reading aloud in class was a source of enjoyment to one and all, for my pronunciation was dreadful and would have the children and teacher convulsed in laughter. I learnt to read and write French a lot better than I could speak the language. A number of the boys, including Jean-Pierre Pugol (whose father was the Administrator of the Marquesas Islands, the tall mountainous group north-east of Tahiti), Philippe Meunier, Jean-Mark Nobholtz and Alain Mouttham, used to devote their lunch periods to improving my French, while they tried to satisfy their insatiable appetite for knowledge of the marine environment. I had so many invitations to visit their homes that I rarely ate alone.

I had left the Matavai Hotel to stay with Gaby Nadeau, the secretary of Monsieur Depierre the headmaster, at her pleasant little home at Pirea. Each day I would travel with Gaby in her car to school. It was an adventurous start. We would hurtle down the narrow, twisting lane that led to the main road at breakneck speed, horn blaring, and careering around assorted chickens, ducks, cats and dogs that were allowed to roam wild by the Tahitians. Once on the main road, Gaby would weave in and out of the heavy morning traffic, oblivious to the string of insults that followed her manoeuvres. It was always with a sense of relief that I found myself at the school gates and we ground to a stop in the parking lot. Gaby never even dented a fender, which I considered a miracle; for while she drove she would often let go the wheel completely to gesticulate at some passing motorist, or to impress upon me some particular point of our conversation. She was a wonderful cook.

Tahitian hospitality and friendliness have long been a legend throughout the Pacific; and now it is the French themselves who excel in these virtues. So genuine was the warmth of the French in all walks of life, from the man in the street to senior Government officials, that I found their hospitality almost embarrassing. The French also have a deep love of the ocean: they were hungry for information about the ways of the sea, its life and its mysteries. It is not by chance that their nation leads the world in oceanographic research, for, realizing the great importance of the future development of the marine resources of the world, it is the French who have pioneered many of the most significant technological advances.

89

One day while walking with Dr Malarde in the Institute grounds, he fell against the wall and I had to help him to his office. I was greatly alarmed, he looked so ill, but he brushed aside my concern with a smile and assured me that he would be all right. Not being convinced, I hurried to Ray Bagnis's office to pour forth my concern.

"So you have noticed at last," Ray said. "Louis is suffering from an incurable form of blood cancer and there is nothing we can do. He is a very brave man."

I was stunned. I had grown attached to this quiet, sincere man, so dedicated to his work, so eager to listen to my research problems and frustrations.

"Does he know?" I asked.

"But of course."

"How long does he have?"

"We do not know—perhaps there will be a new drug—something." Ray gave a typical Frenchman's shrug of the shoulders, but I could see the concern in his face.

Plans were in progress for me to visit the Tuamotus, and I had several long meetings with Monsieur Claude LeBigot, the then head of the Department of Fisheries, and Monsieur Amaru, the head of the Mercantile Marine Department, who were providing the transportation of my equipment into the area. As I was working in close co-operation with the Fisheries Office, Monsieur LeBigot suggested that I establish my research headquarters at Avatoru on Rangiroa Atoll in the Tuamotou Islands, where there were facilities that would help in the research undertaking. A short visit to the atoll established that this indeed was the logical and ideal base for the project. The atoll was serviced twice a week by the R.A.I. Airlines DC-4 flight from Tahiti; there was regular daily radio contact with Papeete; and the airport was also used by the French Airforce on occasional flights.

But there was a problem: the approaching "wet season", when conditions would be far from ideal for research. During the summer months strong, squally northerly winds made the seas rough, and heavy rain added to the unpleasantness.

After discussion with Dr Malarde and the French Administration it was decided to postpone the programme until the following

March or April when the weather would have greatly improved. The project was divided into two six-monthly periods, each during the "dry season" months corresponding to the Australian winter, and was to be extended over 1968 and 1969. I had the choice of remaining in French Polynesia and continuing my schooling (for there was only a short period of school holidays over Christmas and New Year), or returning to Australia. I chose the latter because I knew I would need an assistant for the coming research and wanted to find an Australian. Also, the cost of living in Tahiti was at that time the highest in the world.

I found it amusing that the Tahitians placed such emphasis on their "no tipping" custom: they had little need to seek tips when their charges were so high. Perhaps this was because they were dealing so often with American tourists who seemed to have inexhaustible funds. They were ripe for "touching" as one Chinese merchant told me as he hurried about his shop removing all the price tags.

"What are you doing that for?" I asked.

"An American tourist ship is coming," he replied. "All prices go up while she is in port."

I found it difficult to adjust to Australian ways on my return to Sydney, where I stayed with my parents. Shortly after my arrival, on 24th November 1967, I wrote to the then Prime Minister, the late Harold Holt, outlining my research programme, and pointing out that the co-operation and assistance I was receiving from the French could not possibly be obtained in my own country. I suggested the establishment of a controlling research authority to co-ordinate such activities and simplify the involvement of various Government Departments, with a minimum of red-tape. This the French had managed to do. I pointed out that my research programme in French Polynesia was being assisted by numerous Government and semi-Government Departments—including the Medical Institute, Fisheries, Shipping, Customs, the French Armed Forces—and that to obtain a comparable involvement of Australian Government Departments would be virtually impossible under the present system of control.

On 4th December I had a reply from Mr Holt's secretary, E. J. Bunting, thanking me for my letter and recommendation for the formation of a Research Advisory Panel under the control of the Commonwealth Government. I was advised that the matter was receiving attention, and that the Prime Minister would contact me further as soon as possible.

On Sunday afternoon, 17th December, while I was typing a report in my home at East Lindfield, my mother came hurrying in. "Something terrible has happened," she said. "They think that the Prime Minister has been drowned." I couldn't believe it. But, on turning on the radio, I heard the grim truth for myself. The Prime Minister of Australia, Mr Harold Holt, had disappeared while swimming.

There followed a massive search and there was naturally much speculation as to the cause of Mr Holt's death. I was amazed that the authorities were consistently failing to explore one obvious possible cause of Mr Holt's disappearance: death from shark attack. So strongly did I feel about this that on 20th December I felt compelled to contact the Commissioner of Police of the Victorian State Police Department. I wrote:

> I have hesitated in writing this letter in case the contents are misconstrued by your Department. I wish to make known that I am in no way criticizing your Department, or any Department or organization which has been, or is engaged in the search for the missing Prime Minister.
>
> I do feel, however, that with due regard to the magnitude of the tragedy, every avenue of investigation, no matter how remote, should have been fully dealt with.
>
> I respectfully wish to point out that the possibility of shark attack in this instance could have been more fully investigated. A standard procedure in cases where it is considered possible that a shark fatality may have occurred, is the setting of shark catching equipment, and the subsequent examination of all sharks taken.

The letter went on to point out that the results of my past experimental work indicated that there was a possibility of shark attack in this instance. On 3rd January I received a reply from the Chief Commissioner, R. H. Arnold, saying that "the matter of a shark attack could not have been more fully investigated". But this was obviously not the case, for no attempt had been made to capture and record the stomach contents of any sharks that may have been in the area. The only attempt to examine a shark taken in the locality was made on 22nd December after the Commissioner got my letter—this being sent by special delivery. Inspector L. J. Newell, of the Victorian Police, reported that a Mr Leslie Blackney, a professional fisherman, had killed a large Whaler Shark (a known man-eater) off Point Henry in Corio Bay on 20th December. The police decided to locate this shark and have the contents of the stomach examined; but when Blackney was taken to Corio Bay in a Naval work boat, with police divers and a helicopter, the shark could not be found.

There is evidence to suggest that the late Prime Minister, Harold Holt, was attacked and killed by a shark. He disappeared while swimming at about mid-day on Sunday, 17th December 1967, at Cheviot Beach, Portsea, on the Victorian coast. He was alone in the water at the time.

Witnesses stated that Holt knew the beach like the "back of his hand". The tide was unusually high at the time and the Prime Minister was observed to be swimming quietly, well out from the beach, when the water suddenly became "turbulent" and appeared to boil. It was then that Mr Holt disappeared. Other witnesses stated that they considered the conditions to be very bad and dangerous for swimming at the time.

Mr Theo Scales, a lifelong friend of Harold Holt, said that the Prime Minister was an average swimmer, but had terrific powers of endurance. He had a detailed underwater knowledge of Cheviot Beach, more than any other swimmer known to Scales. Holt had regularly hunted for crayfish in the area, and with seven years' of underwater diving experience was not the type to take risks. Scales said that Holt was fully conscious of his limits when swimming or diving.

Mr Alan Stewart, a witness to the tragedy, said that the Prime Minister's actions on the day of his disappearance when he entered the water to swim were calculated and within his proven ability. Marjorie Gillespie, who was also watching Holt, said, "When I saw him in the water he had his head up at all times and he appeared to be stroking underwater." As Mrs Gillespie continued to watch she noticed that the Prime Minister was still quietly swimming well out, and seemed to be getting farther away all the time. She saw the water become very turbulent around him suddenly. It appeared to "boil", and seemed to "swamp" him Mr Holt was not seen again.

Vyner Gillespie, who was also on the beach at the time, reported that Holt disappeared near the place the locals called the "Blow Hole Pool". She mentioned that the Prime Minister had been wearing tight-fitting black swimming trunks and possibly an old pair of sandshoes when he entered the water.

Neville Woods, a corporal attached to the Officer Cadet School at Portsea, behind which Cheviot Beach is located, was called to the scene a few minutes after Holt's disappearance, by Alan Stewart. Taking a pair of binoculars he hurried to the hill overlooking Cheviot Beach where he made a search of the area. Woods said, "In the Blow Hole Pool I thought I saw something pink in the water, but I couldn't see what it was and I couldn't be sure."

An extensive air and sea search failed to find any trace of the Prime Minister's body. These activities included a thorough and detailed underwater search by divers of the entire locality. It was concluded that Mr Holt had been drowned in the rough conditions prevailing at the time, that his body had been carried away from the locality by the strong undertow, and consumed by marine life.

There were soon wild rumours that the Prime Minister had been assassinated, that he had committed suicide . . . such speculations were completely disproven by the available evidence and subsequent extensive investigations by Commonwealth and State Police.

The evidence to indicate that the Prime Minister was attacked and killed by a shark while swimming is sound.

The Locality. This is frequented by known and reputed man-eating sharks. Species that have been recorded in the immediate vicinity of Holt's disappearance include the dangerous Whaler Shark and the White Shark. Although the White Shark rarely moves into close inshore areas, it has been encountered on a number of occasions in Port Phillip Bay and was responsible for a fatal attack in that region. In attacks on humans by White Sharks the entire victim is carried away, whereas other sharks, such as the Whaler, take a leg or arm first giving the victim the opportunity to call or signal for help. The attacking shark was most likely a White Shark (*Carcharodon carcharias*), seizing the Prime Minister suddenly and dragging him below the surface before he could give any sign.

The Prevailing Conditions. These were ideal for a shark attack, with extremely poor visibility under water. Divers who entered the water immediately afterwards reported visibility at about eight to ten inches. The weather was cloudy and overcast, which would have further reduced the chances of the attacking shark making visual contact with its victim. The fact that the water was turbulent or subject to a strong undertow—one witness mentioned a possible outflowing current in the vicinity of 10 knots—is of little importance. I have observed large sharks "surfing-in" over the fringing coral reefs of an atoll to reach the calm, deep waters of the lagoon. This was despite a heavy and dangerous surf pounding on the corals with destructive force. Underwater rips, currents, undertows, or the most violent turbulence experienced under water along our coastline, would do little to affect or hamper the movements of a shark.

The Time. The tide was high, unusually so, and was at slack water when the Prime Minister entered to swim. It would have started to turn at about the time he disappeared. When a shark is responding to sound vibrations or "distress stimulus", and is being guided to its prey in this manner, the most dangerous period is during slack water on the full tide. This was established beyond doubt during the experimental work entitled "Swimmers in Distress and the Related Effect on the Behaviour Pattern of Sharks".

Blood? At the very spot where the Prime Minister disappeared the witness Corporal Neville Woods thought he saw something pink in the water. This was shortly after Holt vanished, and while the first visual search was being made from the hill overlooking the beach with the aid of binoculars. The Prime Minister was wearing tight-fitting black swim shorts, and was carrying or wearing nothing of a pink colour. What was most likely seen by Corporal Woods from his elevated position was an area of blood, being dissipated through the surrounding water by the currents and turbulence.

The tragic sequence of events which led to Holt's death may be reconstructed: The Prime Minister entered the water for a swim. On finding that he was being carried out in an unexpected undertow, he reacted calmly, and as would be expected of a man with his mental capabilities and attributes, and his experience in swimming. He commenced to swim quietly across the current, for he had a sound knowledge of the entire locality. Upon reaching the area of turbulent water, increased physical exertion was required, and so Holt commenced to unwittingly transmit attractive sound vibrations or "distress stimulus". The shark would have already moved into the immediate locality to investigate the swimmer's movements. Although it appears that Holt was employing a form of breaststroke, he was suffering from the effects of a shoulder disability, and this could have resulted in an erratic or uneven swimming stroke. When last seen the swimmer was holding his head high and swimming strongly, and then suddenly he vanished from sight as the surrounding water "boiled". There was no cry for help, no attempt to signal assistance, not the slightest indication that something was amiss. The shark, already alerted and attracted to the area, immediately responded to the "distress stimulus" and attacked. The Prime Minister was seized by the creature's powerful jaws and was dragged under water before he could do anything. The attacking shark carried the body away from the immediate locality and devoured it.

Many theories were advanced to account for the failure to recover Holt's body. It was argued by fishermen and others (presuming Holt had drowned) that the body would have been completely stripped of flesh within eight to fourteen hours by crayfish and sea lice. The Victorian Government Pathologist, Dr J. H. MacNamara said, "In the event of the body being lodged on the sea floor it would deteriorate rapidly by reason of attack from marine life. Sea lice were prevalent in the waters. The body could be stripped of flesh to the bones within a matter of twenty-four hours." He further pointed out that the body, if not stripped, would rise within twenty to forty-eight hours.

Although what Dr MacNamara said was correct in theory, this rarely occurs in actual practice. During my tours of duty as a police diver in Western Australia and the Northern Territory I was involved in a considerable number of drowning cases dealing with loss of life at sea. The bodies were always recovered and although these bore the marks of attack by small marine creatures they were never "stripped of flesh". I have known bodies to rise to the surface after as long as 120 hours with little visual evidence of assault by marine organisms. Drowning cases I have investigated in tropical regions, where the marine organisms capable of denuding a body of flesh are far more prolific, have usually resulted in a recovery of the missing person, often after some days in the sea. In a number of supposed "drowning" cases there is no subsequent recovery of the body; but it must be borne in mind that there is usually little or no concentrated search for the missing person.

Had Holt's body floated to the surface, which it would have done if he had drowned, it would have been recovered. With such a massive search operation it would have been virtually impossible for a floating body to avoid detection. The theory that the body was swept under by the kelp growing in the area is difficult to accept: the unusually high tide would have tended to lift a swimmer above this, apart from the broken and drifting portions; and the kelp would have tended to "hold' the body in the immediate locality. One only has to don an aqualung and become tangled in kelp to see how difficult it is to escape, even when armed with a sharp diver's knife to cut the weed.

For some reason the authorities responsible for the search operations after the disappearance of the Prime Minister completely ignored the possibility of shark attack. Why was no attempt made to capture sharks known to frequent the area and thus enable an examination of the stomach contents to be made? Even after my letter to the Commissioner on 20th December it was not too late; for often the attacking shark will remain in the locality for some time. The obvious course of action was to employ shark-catching rigs over an area of several miles, centred at Cheviot Beach. But no action was taken.

If the likelihood of shark attack was suppressed to avoid harming the "Australian image", this object was not achieved. While attending an international science congress I casually mentioned my theory of Holt's death, and was immediately told that shark attack had been headlined as the cause of death in many of the countries delegates had come from.

December 1967 was indeed a tragic month for me. After the death of the Prime Minister, a brilliant and dedicated man, I had a letter from Andy Babst telling me that Louis Malarde had died shortly after his return from the Hawiian Islands. I was greatly saddened by the passing of this great man, for he had given his life

97

to the service of others. He had endured to the very last, ignoring his own plight to administer to the needs of his fellows. The name of Dr Louis Malarde was known and loved throughout French Polynesia, and will endure as long as the seas wash the golden shores of the Pacific Islands.

8

My return to French Polynesia was fast approaching, but I was having trouble finding a suitable unpaid research assistant. I was prepared to meet all travel and living expenses for the six month season, but the qualified research assistants who applied for the job all needed a salary as well, and this I could not afford.

I was moaning about my problems to Ronnie Chilcott, my resident North Queensland agent, during a trunk call to Magnetic Island, when she said, "Why not take one of my boys? Robert has just turned fifteen and is dead keen on under water, and is breaking his neck to get away from home for a while; and, besides, he can continue his schooling by correspondence."

So it was arranged, and Robert arrived in Sydney a day or so before my departure for Tahiti. A tall, fair-haired, good-looking lad, deeply sun-tanned by the northern tropical sun, Robert was full of enthusiasm.

Colonel Garnier and Andy Babst were at Papeete airport to welcome us, as were numerous schoolboy friends, who, with one of my teachers, had arranged time off from their classes to greet me. I was soon bedecked with fresh flower and shell leis, the traditional Tahitian welcome, and given the warm French embrace. Ray Bagnis and the new Director of the Medical Institute, Dr Saugrain, who was fresh from France, were also there to welcome me, with many others of the staff, including my close friend Monsieur LeBoucher.

There followed a hectic two weeks in Tahiti, filled with parties and official luncheons and engagements, while I completed arrangements for our stay in the Tuamotus. I was greatly relieved when I finally collapsed into my seat on the DC-4, accompanied by Robert.

Approximately two hundred miles north-east of Tahiti, Rangiroa Atoll is the largest of the group of islands in the Tuamotu Archipelago. There are seventy-eight islands or atolls in the Tuamotu group, the most prominent collection of islands in French Polynesia. These are the true flat, coral atolls, and are distinct from the high volcanic and mountainous islands such as Tahiti, Morea and Bora Bora. Rangiroa Atoll, which in the past has been known as "Dean's Island" and "Vlieger", consists of a number of small coral islets that form the perimeter of a large lagoon. This stretch of water is about forty-two miles in length, with a width of sixteen miles at its widest part, and is said to be the largest natural lagoon in the world. In parts, the lagoon has a depth of over two hundred feet.

The islets forming the perimeter of the lagoon vary considerably in length; some are several miles long, others are no larger than someone's back yard. They occupy a surface area of seventy-five square kilometres, and at the most are only a few feet above sea level, being protected from the surrounding sea by the outer fringing reefs. Access to the lagoon is through two entrance passes, one situated at Avatoru and the other at Tiputa. The 350 inhabitants, mainly Tahitians, who live on the atoll are divided into the two villages at Avatoru and Tiputa. Both the villages are picturesque, and Tiputa has an old-world atmosphere with its crumbling, coral-constructed dwellings and churches dating from the latter part of the nineteenth century. Across the road from one of the churches is a "haunted house", a large old two-storey dwelling with rotting woodwork and creaking doors and shutters. Walking past this house one night, I was struck by its sinister appearance, in the pale moonlight that shafted down between the drifting clouds. Perhaps there is good reason to call it the "haunted house": no one has lived beneath its roof for many a year and it is still filled with old decaying furniture.

The atoll is beautiful, with its coconut-palm covered islands and rich tropical vegetation. Massive breadfruit trees grow wild, as do pawpaw and banana trees; and with these and the wealth of marine life in the lagoon one can comfortably live off the land. On our arrival at Rangiroa, Robert and I were taken to stay with Mama and Papa Iterma, a pleasant Tahitian couple. With their two boys, Didia and Eipoo, they lived at Avatoru. Our quarters provided by the Fisheries Department were not yet ready, so we spent a pleasant few weeks with the family. Papa was a fisherman who had several traps in the lagoon, and despite the handicap of having only one arm he was one of the hardest working and most successful Tahitians on the atoll.

Papa had lost his arm to a shark. One day, while clearing his traps of several sharks with the aid of a harpoon, he attempted to spear a Grey Shark, or "Raira", as it is called by the locals. His harpoon pierced the back of the shark, and Papa was pulled off the side of his trap into the water where he was immediately attacked and lost his arm. A lesser man would have died long before the arrival of the plane from Tahiti which was sent to take him to the closest hospital in Papeete. But Papa survived and was soon back at work on his traps, undaunted by his loss.

The Tahitian population, like Papa, is self-supporting, and engages in fishing and in collecting copra from the fallen coconuts. No one works very hard, apart from Papa, and the fishing potential of the lagoon and surrounding waters is virtually untouched. The lagoon has one of the most prolific assortments of marine life in the greatest abundance I have seen anywhere. It is truly a fisherman's paradise. Fishing is simple, and I would see Robert with an old fishing-line with several hooks attached, a piece of broken coral for a sinker, lower his "rig" to the lagoon floor and then immediately haul in one or more good-sized fish. While we speeded across the lagoon in a boat, the water ahead would sometimes start to turn black, and soon we would be surrounded on every side by acres and acres of schooling fish. Robert and I have donned our diving equipment and dived down into the lagoon amongst the school. The first forty feet or so was just a solid wall of moving fish, an unbelievable sight, countless millions of them milling about, completely unafraid of our presence, for a sudden movement in the school would send them crashing and thumping against our bodies.

Visibility under water was usually good, with moderately clear water, particularly on the incoming tide in the vicinity of the entrance passes, where the water would become crystal clear. But experienced divers who have visited the atoll say that the diving conditions when working the entrance passes are the most dangerous in the world. Here the currents would often exceed ten knots and their direction was completely unpredictable.

Shortly after my arrival, I decided to "depth" the Avatoru entrance pass at its deepest point. The flow had ceased, and normally I had thirty minutes diving time with a minimum of danger from excessive water movement. I reached about 75 feet and could see that I had another 20 feet or so to go before I reached the floor of the pass. This had been washed clean by the enormous rush of water sweeping into and out of the lagoon. There was no coral, just nothing, only a smooth pavement of tightly packed coral rubble. As I moved down through the remaining few feet of water I was seized by a sudden current and whirled about. It was as though some gigantic hand had hold of me and was forcing me through the water. I fought to the bottom and tried to find a finger hold, but I was being forced along backwards at an ever-increasing rate. Realizing that it was useless to try to resist the enormous pressure of water that was bearing down on me, I headed for the surface. Half-way up the current suddenly ceased and the water was still. I was just congratulating myself when my facemask was whipped from my face and I was spun around at such a speed I became dizzy. Then I was being forced back the way I had just come, the pressure of water roaring in my ears.

I had had enough, and without even attempting to replace my facemask with the spare always carried on my belt, I inflated my safety vest and shot to the surface. Here the water was calm once more. There was no warning of the dangerous turbulence below.

The two passes are narrow and deep and, depending on the direction of the flood, the rushing waters build up into a dangerous maelstrom at either end. In rough weather the wildness of the water is truly awesome to behold, for the opposing waves generated by the tumbling current and the prevailing wind meet in violent confusion, flinging spray and spume high into the air and making a thunderous roar. For a diver to enter the maelstrom at such a time would be fatal. Even a large launch could not move into this torrent of disturbed water in safety; the opposing waves would quickly swamp it or lift it from the water and cast it aside, overturned or broken. Even on the calmest of days these passes were a hazard. When the flow reached its peak the rushing, twisting waters would form deep pockets or eddies that would suck a swimmer down.

And it was here that the greatest number of sharks were to be found, particularly when the current was rushing into the lagoon. The sharks would gather at the lagoon end of the pass, sometimes hundreds at a time, to wait for the fish and animals that came shooting down the pass on the incoming tide.

An American camera crew, I was told, had visited the atoll to make an underwater film on sharks. Equipped with diving gear, they had "shot the pass". Sweeping into the maelstrom area, they had been confronted by a solid wall of sharks, some hundreds of them. One American was afterwards taken from the atoll in a state of mental shock, so terrifying had the sight been.

Robert and I were often to shoot the pass during the coming months, but we did not allow the current to carry us into the maelstrom. We would take one side of the pass and sweep into the lagoon to the right or the left of the treacherous current. And we did this only when the waters were rushing into the lagoon; for to have attempted it when the tide had turned and the water was being forced out of the lagoon into the ocean would have been certain death. On the outgoing tide the enormous mass of water spills over the edge of the surrounding coral reefs into deep water, sucking everything down with it to a depth of hundreds of feet.

We would don our diving equipment and, followed by a Tahitian in a boat, would plunge down into the swirling current to be plucked effortlessly along as if by some gigantic hand. The corals on the side of the pass would rush by in a confused blur as we gathered speed and were swept down along the pass. It was an exhilarating experience, perhaps the closest that a man can ever approach to free flight. And then suddenly we would be carried round the corner and far out into the lagoon, where the dying current would leave us and we would clamber back into the waiting boat.

It was the first of May 1968 when Robert and I arrived at

Rangiroa, and the rains had long since departed. My equipment was not expected for some days, and I was impatient to start, for the weather was glorious. The brilliant tropical sun beat down on the glassy smooth waters from a cloudless sky, and there was not a breath of wind. The deep blue of the lagoon blended with that of the sky, and where they met there was no horizon, just nothing. Speeding across the lagoon in a boat we appeared to be floating or flying through the air. It was only when there was a sudden ripple on the surface, perhaps caused by some fish, that one would be jerked back to reality and the hypnotic spell broken.

The day after our arrival Papa and his friend Theodore Cadousteau, the young Tahitian in charge of the Fisheries post at Avatoru, agreed to take us out into the maelstrom area when conditions were safe. It was about two in the afternoon and, accompanied by the rest of the Fisheries staff, we set off in two outboard-powered boats. Alexis Teiva, or Jumbo as he came to be affectionately known to Robert and me, and the "Little Bloke" sped alongside us in the other boat. Jumbo was a tall, heavily built Tahitian, and like most large men was immediately friendly and helpful. "The Little Bloke", for I have never called him anything else and still do not know his name, was small and wiry and made me think of a bantam rooster. Drinking beer was the favourite pastime of half the Tahitians on the atoll, and he loved his beer. Whenever the opportunity for a "party" arose the Little Bloke would be there; but not Jumbo, Theodore or Papa who rarely, if ever, indulged. It took very little alcohol to put the Tahitians under the table, and the local beer was weak compared to the Australian brew. One whiff of the Aussie stuff would have been sufficient to send them staggering on their way.

We soon arrived at the end of the pass and nosed our boats into the deceptive calm. The waters were crystal clear and no more than 20 to 30 feet deep in the centre of the whirlpool, with lush coral growths I had not expected to see in such turbulent waters. On the far side of the maelstrom the corals sloped downwards to about 50 feet or so, and here, on the pure white sand that was dotted with massive coral bombies, were the sharks.

As I entered the water I counted twenty-eight sharks moving about in the clear water below me. Robert soon followed, and on taking one look beneath him hastily returned to the boat. He had

Robert prepares to dive with one of the transducers during a sudden
tropical downpour

Surrounded by a mass of cable, Robert places the transducer on the lagoon floor

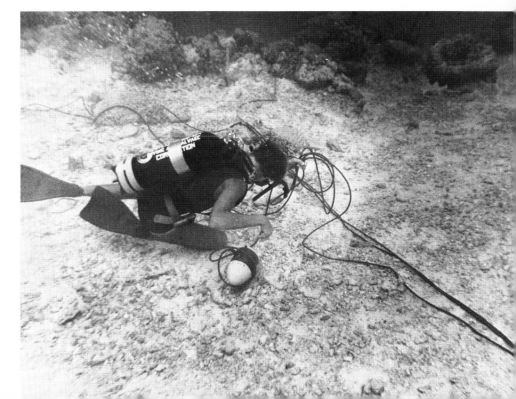

The three transducers are set on the edge of the lagoon entrance pass ready for the next experiment

Dr Bruce Halstead examines a venomous Stone Fish

Dr Don Nelson experiments with underwater sounds on several sharks in a tank

Taking blood samples during the dissecting of sharks at Rangiroa

These young sharks were ready for birth when removed from the mother during dissection

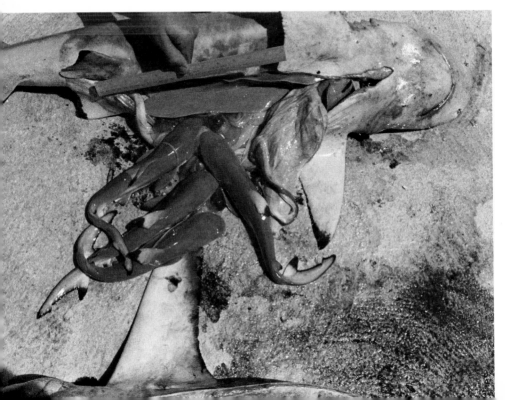

A school of Barracuda attracted by underwater sound transmission. These fish are 6 feet or more in length

One of the many schools of fish that make Rangiroa Atoll a fisherman's paradise

A deadly sea snake found swimming amongst bathers at Port Moresby's Ela Beach

A huge Manta Ray swims into the test area in Rangiroa lagoon

Sharks attracted by distress stimulus work themselves into a frenzy looking for the signal source

Sharks in a frenzied state fight to reach the source of the attractive signals. Most are obscured by the fine sand that clouds the surrounding water from the lagoon floor

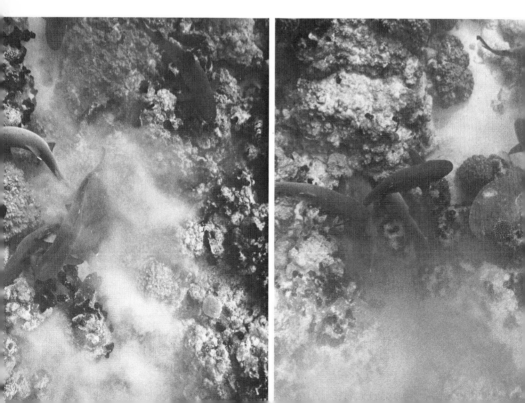

As the fine sand settles sharks that have battered themselves to death in the cave concealing the transducer become visible

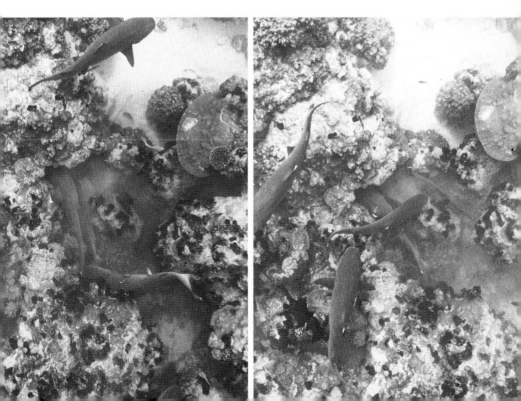

Student trainee Peter Cox makes the outline of the native rock carvings more distinct with the aid of salt

Watched by Tahitian children, divers prepare to dive in the lagoon entrance pass

The author examines a small sea turtle held by Dr Bruce Halstead

Dr Glen Egstrom attaches electrodes to diver Gene Cornelius to record his underwater reactions to sharks

Preparing to dive in the lagoon entrance pass with underwater motion
film camera

Student trainee research assistant Michael O'Leary, of Magnetic Island, peers through the jaws of a large Tiger Shark captured near the island

Robert swims back to the boat with a shark recovered from the set chain lines on the lagoon floor

Another shark specimen killed with an explosive "bang-stick" is taken back to the boat by Robert

Joy Halstead collects marine specimens from the lagoon floor at Rangiroa

Dr Bruce Halstead and assistants gather marine specimens from the lagoon. Much of this work must be done after dark

never seen a shark before, let alone, as he later said, "a platoon of the flamin' things swimming about". But curiosity soon got the better of him and, after watching the rest of us swim about unharmed for some time, Robert was soon at my side.

Papa spied a large fish and dived down to spear it. As he lined up his gun, Jumbo and the Little Bloke dived down to keep the sharks at bay. It was a perfect shot, but the fish, being a large one, dived beneath the coral before Papa could control it. Without hesitating, Papa commenced to wrench it free from the coral, now surrounded by milling sharks. At last the fish came away, and as I watched the drama 50 feet below from the safety of the surface I saw a White-tip Shark move in quickly to snatch the fish. Papa thrust his flipper into the charging shark's head and kicked it away. This was done without fear or concern, just as one would kick an annoying dog from around one's legs. Papa had nothing but contempt for sharks. The fish was soon in the boat, to be followed by several more. As each was speared the Tahitian diver sped to the surface, with the fish dangling well below him on the end of the spear shaft and line. Sometimes a hungry shark would rush up after the wriggling, wounded catch, and would snatch the fish from the spear. There would be laughter and excited cries in Tahitian of "Maamaa ma'o, maamaa ma'o", meaning crazy shark, crazy shark. Soon the sharks attracted to the area by the struggling fish, had become too numerous to count. They drifted about below, their dark and sinister bodies silhouetted against the sparkling white sand. Never did they attempt to molest us on the surface, and only when a fish was speared did they become hostile to the diver down below, and then it was the catch that they were after. The sharks in Australia and New Guinea often follow the diver to the surface and track him like a hungry dog; but not so here. The sharks appeared to avoid the upper layers of their domain.

"Papu ore, ta ia," cried our Tahitian friends together as the first pull of the rising current was felt against our bodies. It was now unsafe to stay, they were telling us, and it was with difficulty that we swam against the stream to our boats.

Mama and Papa had many dogs, and so did every other Tahitian on the atoll, it seemed. It was not unusual to see a massive dog fight involving dozens of yapping, snarling animals; but a boot in the tail would send the largest and most ferocious scurrying on its way. Robert had names for all Mama's dogs, and these included Nero—who was quite mad and would stand in the water barking furiously at nothing in particular for hours, Flavius, Octavius, Caesar, Mark Antony, and Cleopatra, to mention just a few. During our stay at Mama's Robert would often come to me and say, "Have you seen Octavius—or so and so—he has vanished and I can't find him anywhere." But I had too many problems to be worried about dogs.

During meal-time it was necessary to hunt the dogs, cats and assorted other livestock from the house so that we could eat in peace. Mama was a wonderful cook, and the meals she prepared, which always included fresh fish from Papa's traps, were delicious. It was not uncommon for Mama to seize the first available object from the table and fling this towards the door, as "Pooer" the pig or some other animal attempted to make an untimely entrance.

There was much excitement at the village when the French Government boat arrived with my equipment. This was soon unloaded; but on checking the equipment I found that one of my brand-new and best high-performance tape-recorders was wrecked beyond repair. Everything else appeared in perfect condition after the long trip from Papeete via numerous small islands and atolls. It was fortunate that the Fisheries outpost had its own power supplies, so that when Robert and I were stationed there we could work from our own backyard. The Fisheries depot was pleasantly located by the side of the Avatoru lagoon entrance pass, and so close to the water was the main building that I could set up my transmitting equipment under the shade of the tropical trees next to our room. From here it was possible to "call-in" sharks to the shallow waters on the side of the pass, a few yards from where we slept.

But disaster was soon to strike; an unbelievable series of misfortunes was to wreck the entire research season. I was equipped with electronic gear direct from the manufacturers, brand-new and completely tested. When I checked the two main amplification units, the most vital pieces of equipment that increased the signal strength to the level required, one unit failed immediately and had to be air-freighted to Tahiti for repairs. Then, during the first series of field experiments, the second amplifier also failed, and burnt out several resistors and other components. This also was rushed to Tahiti for repairs, and I was fortunate to get the first amplifier back so that work could proceed. Then, while I was engaged in the next series of field experiments, the audio-signal generator, the piece of equipment that generated the pure signal tones required for the repellent programme, also played up. The signal output control failed, and the resulting surge of signal power burnt out the remaining amplifier. All were packed up and sent off to Tahiti, and while I waited for the repairs to be carried out I commenced to experiment with the recording of "distress stimulus" and the overlaying of one signal pattern on another. But here again I was foiled. My hydrophone flooded, and when the stand-by underwater microphone was used it leaked.

I finally managed to repair the hydrophone. Papa had given me the use of his trap, which was full of fish, to record a new type of "distress stimulus" signal pattern I was experimenting with. Everything was positioned in our boat alongside Papa's trap, I started the generator and began to record the signals I was seeking. This was being accomplished beautifully: the noise levels were perfect and exactly what I required. Then the generator stopped. It was brand-new and had operated for under five minutes before it failed. I just couldn't believe it. It must be some sort of a bad dream. No one could have such bad luck. But the generator never ran again. There was a fault in the valves, and it was replaced on my return to Australia.

My amplification units were too complex for the radio repair shops at Papeete to handle, and on their return I suffered almost immediate failure. Parts were not available, and there were long delays while these were obtained. The repair costs were enormous, and soon I was facing a serious financial crisis. The high cost of air freight to and from Tahiti aggravated the critical situation. In desperation I wrote to the Australian Prime Minister, Mr John Gorton, asking for the loan of further high-performance electronic recording equipment to enable the programme to continue. I wrote to the Pioneer Electronic Corporation asking for replacement amplification units, and to many other equipment manufacturers whose items had failed. All avenues of assistance were explored. Only the Pioneer Electronic Corporation of Japan came to my immediate assistance, dispatched by air-freight, without charge, another new amplifier from their Tokyo office. There were negative replies to all my other requests.

At the height of my troubles I had a letter from my father to say that my mother had died a few days before. It was many days before I cared about anything. I had been close to my mother, and it was unbearable to know that she had gone, that she wouldn't be waiting for me when I went home. Everything seemed empty and meaningless. But in the days that followed I fought back the depression that threatened to engulf me. I couldn't give up now; I had to carry on to the end.

Dr Yues B. Plessis, of the Paris Museum of Natural History, was a jovial man, and he came to stay with Mama and Papa just before we moved into our new quarters. He was collecting specimens of fish from the lagoon and preserving these for shipment back to Paris. He spoke enough English for us to communicate in comfort, for I was still not very capable with my French. When he heard of my problems he was most sympathetic and immediately set about helping me. He arranged for the French warship *Forbin* to take my defunct equipment on board, there to be examined by the electronic engineers on board; for Dr Plessis was also involved with the French Atomic Energy Commission. Shortly before the *Forbin* sailed from its anchorage in the lagoon at Tiputa, my equipment was returned in working order.

Dr Plessis watched while Robert and I enthusiastically checked the equipment on our arrival back at Avatoru. It was functioning perfectly, and we amused ourselves by transmitting high-frequency signals at the Tahitian girls cleaning fish ready for shipment.

"Will we call some sharks in this afternoon?" asked Robert, as we prepared to pack up the equipment.

"No," I said, "we will leave it for tomorrow."

As I spoke there was a puff of blue smoke from the amplifier and, with a strangled screech, the equipment went dead.

"Impossible!" exclaimed Dr Plessis as he surveyed the still smoking amplifier. "Impossible!" he repeated as he wrung his hands and walked away. But the impossible had happened again. The unit had burnt out.

The following day Dr Plessis and I went across the lagoon with Desire Heuea (or Jules as he preferred to be known) in his speed boat. Dr Plessis had hired Jules, the Tahitian policeman at Avatoru, to take him to the opposite side of the lagoon known as the Sector area. We were to collect specimens, for Dr Plessis required a few more fish before he returned to Tahiti the next day. It was a glorious morning, and I soon forgot my problems as we glided over the glistening waters of the lagoon. Ahead, Dr Plessis pointed to several huge manta rays, swimming like gigantic bats through the water close to the surface. Jules chased one of the beasts, which must have been over fifteen feet across, but it soon dived out of sight. We arrived at a picturesque lagoon within a lagoon, a small stretch of water completely surrounded by tiny coconut-covered islets. Dr Plessis set his nets in the knee-deep water and began to drive fish into the trap. Soon several small sharks arrived, and darted at the fish already caught in the nets. More sharks appeared of the small White-tip and Black-tip Reef variety. As Dr Plessis splashed through the water the sharks were attracted to him, and soon he was being followed by a train of small fins. The faster he moved, the more he splashed, and the more the sharks responded and chased him. "Stand still," I yelled. "They will go away." But Dr Plessis was having none of it, and he bounded up onto a large piece of coral and stood surveying his tormentors. These soon disappeared and we went on with the work. Jules prepared cool freshly picked green coconuts for lunch, and we drank the refreshing milk while we munched contentedly on sweet biscuits, sitting under the shady palms.

Andy Babst sounded angry when his voice floated over the radio.

"Why on earth didn't you let me know you were in trouble? That's what we are here for. Monsieur LeBigot is flying down to Rangiroa tomorrow morning in a special flight to see you. He is to pick up your equipment for repairs at the Naval workshop in Tahiti. A shipment of stores is already on its way to you. Is there anything else you require?"

I was too surprised to reply immediately and said weakly, "How did you know?"

"Dr Plessis called at my office this morning as soon as he arrived back in Papeete," came Andy's hurt voice. "If you need anything else please contact me immediately by radio—and that's an order."

"Good old Andy," cried Rob when he heard the wonderful news. "It will be a change to have something else but fish for tea."

During the next few weeks while we waited for the return of our equipment, Robbie and I concentrated on catching sharks for specimen study and for tagging purposes. Dr Perry Gilbert had given me a number of the stainless steel shark tags used by the American Institute of Biological Sciences for their Shark Research Panel work. These were numbered and, with the aid of an applicator, were attached to the back of the first dorsal fin at its base. The object was to mark as many sharks as possible in this manner before they were released, so that the migratory habits of both the lagoon and pelagic species employed for the work could be studied, as well as their rate of growth, the size and age they attained, and so on. Persons catching the tagged sharks were requested to remove the identification marker and return it together with all possible data: where the animal was captured, how long it was, and other relevant facts. In 1964 Perry Gilbert had spent a month at the neighbouring atoll of Tikehau, a few miles to the south of Rangiroa, where he had tagged a number of sharks during the course of his research. I was hoping to catch one of Perry's tagged sharks, but this was not to happen.

Each evening I would set out heavy shark-catching rig in the lagoon and at the ocean end of the Avatoru entrance pass. One afternoon, after renewing the baited hooks, Robert and I decided to fish in the entrance pass opposite the Fisheries outpost. There was little current when we anchored, and we soon had more than sufficient fish to meet our needs, and so agreed to return for our tea. But the anchor was stuck fast on the bottom of the pass and even with the aid of the motor I was unable to free it. After about thirty minutes of fruitless manoeuvring, the Little Bloke paddled out in a canoe to where we were anchored. The current had turned and was now moving out to sea at some speed, so I decided. that Robert should return to the shore in the canoe. This he did, arriving safely and waving to us from the jetty. I was loath to cut the rope, for this was new and over 150 feet in length, and the anchor belonged to Theodore. But after a further fifteen minutes or so, even with the aid of the Little Bloke, I was still unable to budge the thing, so I decided it must go.

The current was now rushing seawards at considerable speed, and it was fast approaching dusk as I reached for the knife. "No, no, one more time," cried the Little Bloke. As he spoke he revved the motor and the boat shot ahead into the current, but before the Little Bloke could act the boat was spun around crazily by the rushing water and the anchor rope caught over the stern. The pressure from the current quickly pulled the stern under water, and I can remember running up the side of the tipping boat and stepping into the water as the boat disappeared with alarming speed.

I looked around but the boat had gone, dragged down by the tremendous force of the rushing water as it fought against the restraining anchor line. So had the Little Bloke, and I could do nothing with the current now raging at 10 knots or more. I knew if I couldn't reach the side of the lagoon pass before I was swept into the maelstrom I was finished, and it soon became apparent that I could never make it, for I was being whirled along at an ever-increasing speed. And then suddenly, about a hundred yards behind me, up popped the Little Bloke, and then the waterlogged boat.

Later I was to learn from the Little Bloke that he had become tangled and caught under the boat as it plunged downwards. Somehow he managed to find the knife, which was still inside, and had cut himself free, and then cut the anchor line. The boat had drifted upwards again, for it was supported with inbuilt floatation tanks.

I swam against the current and the rapidly moving boat was soon alongside. We looked at each other and out at the maelstrom. There was just nothing we could do. The waves were foaming white, and I could hear the thunderous roar as the two opposing forces fought each other with relentless fury.

"Papa come, Papa come," cried the Little Bloke above the rising din, and on turning I could see two speedboats bearing down on us.

"Too late," I thought, for it was almost dark and already we were being tossed about by the rising waves.

One of my heavy nylon fishing-lines of over 200-lb. breaking strain was bobbing alongside the boat. I pulled at it but found the line was firmly caught underneath. As Papa drew close I dragged myself up out of the water and threw the heavy plastic reel into his boat. Papa was alone, but he managed to seize the line and quickly made this fast as he backed his boat away. We held our breath as the line took the strain and snapped taut—it held, but we didn't move. Papa increased the power of his straining motor: it seemed hopeless, for we were now on the very edge of the maelstrom. We were being tossed about as the raging current tore at our bodies, trying desperately to pry us loose from the wildly pitching boat. The noise was deafening; spray and spume all but blinded us, and made breathing difficult. Grimly we hung onto our perilous perch while Papa fought to drag us clear.

"The damn fishing-line must break," I thought as it vibrated under the enormous strain.

But then dimly through the rapidly fading light and blinding spray I could see the second boat cautiously approaching, the two Tahitians hanging on grimly as their boat was flung about like a cork in the raging waters. As they swept close to us the man in the bow cast a rope to the Little Bloke. This he was able to seize and quickly made it fast to the end of the anchor rope.

Under the combined power of the two straining motors we were gradually pulled away from that awful cauldron of foaming water. It was dark when the Little Bloke and I were able to drag ourselves into Papa's boat, exhausted and thankful to be alive. Our exploit is still talked about to this very day by the villagers: we had cheated the maelstrom.

One morning Robbie woke me, saying, "The heavy rig has gone."

"Ah, bull," I replied as I rubbed the sleep from my eyes. "Nothing could shift that." But when I dragged myself to the door and looked down the lagoon pass I was instantly awake, for there was nothing.

We had set the heavy rig out several days before, and only the night before I had rebaited the two huge six-inch hooks with massive chunks of flesh from a huge Eagle Ray we had taken from Papa's trap. The baits weighed between 50 and 100 pounds, and the hooks were such that each could support the weight of a large truck of several tons or more. Attached to the hooks were lengths of heavy galvanized chain, and then 30 feet of new 2½-inch nylon rope. This huge rig was supported by two steel-banded 50-gallon drums and anchored by 150 feet of heavy nylon rope, massive chains and swivels, and several blocks of brain coral weighing 200 pounds or more each. It had taken Jumbo and several others, including Rob and myself, all our effort to set up this massive rig. The rope alone could withstand several tons' strain, and not even the rushing current in the pass could hope to shift it.

The weather had been calm overnight and the sea was flat and without a ripple as we started off in the Fisheries boat with Theodore. We searched well out to sea, and then miles down the side of the atoll to follow the course of the prevailing drift; but there was no trace. To satisfy myself, I later checked the floor of the entrance pass in case the drums had been smashed and sunk; but, as I expected, there was nothing. Even the Tahitians were impressed, for it was obvious that some gigantic animal had taken the bait, and then with unbelievable strength had carried everything far away and out to sea. Other heavy rig was later to disappear in a like manner, and when I discussed the matter with Jean Tapu, the famed Tahitian spearfisherman and former world champion of the 1964 Cuba Spearfishing Titles, he was not surprised. Jean was visiting Rangiroa for the Fisheries Department, in Papeete where he worked, and was most interested in my research programme. He told me how many years before his father had talked of a gigantic White Shark he and his father (Jean's grandfather) had seen while journeying between the atolls in their canoe. It had been a monstrous thing, and had lain in the water and watched them pass. Perhaps I was indeed close to the domain of the legendary Great White Shark.

9

While shooting the pass one day, Robert and I noticed a family of seven White-tip Reef Sharks that had established their domicile or "house area" at the lagoon end of the pass. During the following months we observed and recorded the behaviour of the sharks, for it was most unusual to find them with so well-defined a territorial claim.

The sharks lived where the rushing waters of the pass were parted by a small and picturesque palm-covered island, the main stream tumbling into the maelstrom, and the lesser flow on the other side sweeping into the lagoon. The sharks never ventured more than a hundred yards or so from a depression in the floor of the pass, where they had their home. The current had swept the area clean, and it had a desolate and barren appearance, with the steeply sloping sides of the pass towering over the underwater landscape to a height of 75 feet or more. But the sharks fared well on the abundance of fish life sweeping past on their journey into the lagoon.

The family of sharks never moved from their domicile during the months when I recorded their behaviour. The only time they could be enticed from their lair was when "distress stimulus" signals were employed to attract them. If a diver moved towards the depression in the pass floor the sharks would become quite aggressive, and showed a marked territorial-ownership pattern of behaviour. This sense of ownership could account for some attacks on humans, when a diver or swimmer entered the domicile area and the shark retaliated by attacking the intruder. My observations were interrupted when a Tahitian friend arrived from Tahiti and eliminated several of the sharks with his explosive-headed speargun. He disliked sharks, and would hunt them down relentlessly. I arranged for Papa to take this hunter out to the maelstrom area; but when he saw what was gathered there he thought it more prudent to pursue his favourite pastime elsewhere.

Robert and I were in business again and were having success with the experiments designed to attract or call-in sharks. I had decided to concentrate on this aspect of the research programme, since little time was left. The results were quite amazing, and perhaps I was the first man ever to gain some measure of control over sharks in a feeding frenzy.

The species of sharks I was finding in the lagoon were basically identical to those elsewhere in the Pacific. The most dangerous and aggressive of these was the Grey Shark (*Carcharhinus ambly-rhynchos*) which, although smaller than the Australian Whaler, was closely related to it. The Bronze Whaler was occasionally seen, as were large Tigers and Hammerheads. The smaller reef varieties were abundant, the Black-tip Reef Shark (*Carcharhinus melanopterus*) and the White-tip Reef Shark (*Triaenodon obesus*) being the most common. However, the White-tip, unlike its Australian counterpart, grew to over seven feet, and was a particularly aggressive animal, dangerous when stimulated by attractive sound vibrations. Once while swimming in the lagoon I met an unusual shark that appeared to have only four gill openings—an unheard of thing. When I next wrote to Perry Gilbert I mentioned my find. But later, when a nine-foot specimen was caught, it turned out to be the harmless Nurse Shark (*Nebrius doldi*) affectionately known to the Tahitians as "Nohipiri". In this shark the fourth and fifth gills employed the one gill opening. An occasional Lemon Shark (*Negaprion acutidens*) was taken on my catching rig, and outside the lagoon in the deep water I had the misfortune to encounter a White Shark.

This animal was sighted while I was experimenting with a new signal pattern of attractive sounds, which I later loosely termed "stampede distress stimulus", for want of a better name. It consisted of sounds recorded while a massive school of fish were under attack from predators. I was about a mile offshore, and had chosen the area because a number of small birds were circling just above the surface of the water. Their presence often indicated tuna or other large fish. Leaving Robert in the boat to operate the equipment, I went overboard into the cool, dark waters. At about fifty feet I signalled Robert via the buzzer to commence the attractive signals, and within a matter of seconds a White Shark, a massive animal around fifteen feet in length, appeared. Strangely the shark was followed by a school of tuna. I immediately signalled Robert to cease all transmission and watched apprehensively as the White Shark, apparently no longer interested in my presence, moved off into the surrounding gloom. When I quickly surveyed the area I found that the tuna had likewise left, and I lost little time in surfacing and regaining the boat. The outcome of this short experiment was not without interest, for it appeared that the tuna had also responded to the new attractive signal patterns under investigation.

The Tahitians had no fear of the sharks that frequented their lagoon. I have seen small naked children running and jumping off the jetty at Avatoru while sharks cruised close by. They would excitedly call "Ma'o, ma'o" as they played about in the water. Perhaps because of the enormous amount of natural food available, the lagoon sharks were just not aggressive towards humans: the same swimming behaviour in other localities of the Pacific would have had fatal results. Of all the lagoon sharks only "Raira" or the Grey Shark commanded respect. If one of these animals put in an appearance and moved towards the jetty, the children would scuttle from the water and yell insults at the shark until it moved away.

It was not possible to spearfish in the lagoon without being virtually surrounded by sharks. As soon as a fish was speared and started to struggle violently, the sharks would rush in like hungry dogs, snapping at the catch. But never did they molest the spear-fishermen, and the Tahitians merely pushed the sharks away with their flippered feet to protect their catch. But they could always judge the mood of the milling sharks, and when the sharks became excited the Tahitians would leave the wounded fish hanging on the end of their spears as they sped to the surface and safety. Often when I was working at a depth of perhaps 50 feet or more, down would swim Papa or Jumbo to sit on the sea floor at my side, completely oblivious to their surroundings as they watched my work.

My experiments in the maelstrom were awe-inspiring, for I was now able to work sharks into a frenzy at the flick of a switch. On one such occasion a huge number of sharks, perhaps a hundred or more, responded and commenced to mill around the large brain coral under which I had concealed the transducer. Water visibility was perfect, the incoming current having cleared the water to such an extent that I could see 300 feet in any direction. I floated on the surface of the water and watched the excited sharks below. A Harpu cod of around 15 pounds swam towards the corals over the glistening white sand. Without warning, it was suddenly attacked and seized by a White-tip Shark, which then attempted to flee with its struggling prey. This was the signal for the orgy to start, and the sharks exploded into a frenzy of activity. They simultaneously rushed the White-tip and converged into a circular ball of whirling, viciously snapping animals. It was an incredible sight, and there was an audible roar such as would be made by a distant express train as it thundered over a metal bridge. I could see open jaws furiously tearing at flesh, twisting and ripping at anything in sight. Sharks rushed from every direction to join the mêlée, and within a matter of seconds two hundred or more sharks were locked in a life-and-death struggle. They formed one solid mass of living and dying muscle and flesh, completely oblivious to pain and no longer responding to the primitive instinct of survival.

All transmission had ceased, for I had long since signalled Rob, who was controlling the electronic equipment from the safety of the boat. Within perhaps three to five seconds, certainly no more, the White-tip Shark was completely devoured. Nothing remained, for later when I inspected the pure white sands below I could find no trace—not even a tooth or a small shred of flesh. So rapidly had the animal been consumed that no blood had been left to discolour the surrounding water. I was astounded as I watched this display of uncontrolled power and brute force. Jumbo and Jules, who were with me, excitedly called, "Yooooooooo Hoooooooooo ma'o, ma'o", through the water.

And then suddenly they were gone. As if responding to some secret signal, the entire assembly of sharks fled the area. The speed of their disappearance was magical. On the sea floor far below all was quiet and still. A few White-tip Sharks milled about aimlessly, slowly swimming about the corals. It made me feel that what I had seen was an impossible dream.

It was August and the delegates of the South Pacific Commission Conference on Ichthyosarcotoxism, or more simply toxic fish poisoning, had arrived at Rangiroa for the day. Scientists from all over the world had gathered in French Polynesia for the seminar, and among them were Gilbert Whitley and Dr Broadbent from Australia, Dr Hashimoto and Dr Abe from Japan, and many other American, French and British researchers. Dr Saugrain and Ray Bagnis from the Medical Institute were there, and I was advised that I was to return with the delegates to Tahiti on the chartered DC-4, there to attend the week-long conference.

The scientists were first shown the toxic fish exhibits gathered from the lagoon, as well as the sharks Robert and I had captured especially for the occasion. The delegates inspected my research equipment, and I addressed them on its mode of application and the aims of my research. Many of the senior scientists attending the seminar were greatly interested, and particularly Dr Bruce W. Halstead, the world's leading authority on poisonous and venomous marine animals, and the director of the United States Government-sponsored World Life Research Institute, of Colton, California. Afterwards he took me to one side. "Boy, you really have something there. Can you give me a practical demonstration of your work?"

This I immediately agreed to, and so impressed was Bruce that I was quickly appointed an associate of the Institute on his return to California. Then came much needed financial assistance, and so began my association with Dr Halstead and World Life.

Before returning to Tahiti we all went to Tiputa village for a massive lunch. This consisted of freshly caught and cooked crayfish from the lagoon, as well as huge helpings of curried meat and vegetables. Both Robbie and I ate heartily, for meat to us was a rare delicacy, since we had so much fish during our stay on Rangiroa. Leaving Robbie in Jumbo's care, I left for Tahiti and the conference.

The following morning, which was Monday and the start of the seminar, I was talking to several of the American scientists, including Bruce.

"Do the Tahitians eat dog at Rangiroa?" I was asked.

"Not as far as I know," I replied. "Why?"

"Well, boy, you sure ate dog yesterday at Tiputa. That curried meat was good old canine."

I was staggered as Bruce explained how, on completing their meal, some of the scientists had been sifting through the left-over bones, and had recognized them as belonging to dogs. On thinking back, I remembered Rob's concern from time to time at the unexplained disappearance of one of Mama's dogs, and how this always preceded the rare treat of fresh meat on the atoll. But I had enjoyed the food, as I had the turtle meat, the flesh of seabirds, or whatever else Mama had dished up to us. As Robert later remarked, "If that was doggie it sure tasted good!"

During my stay in Papeete Bruce and I spent much time discussing my future plans for the sonic approach to shark repellents. Bruce realized that the experimental programme could yield significant results in other, perhaps equally important, fields. These included the use of underwater sound transmission in the field of commercial fishing. Already field experimental work had indicated that it might be possible to attract certain species of bony fish, including commercial school varieties, to pre-selected localities. This would be of extreme value in the future exploitation of the ocean's resources; and perhaps controlled "fish farming" would soon become a reality, with the fishermen "calling-in" their catch to the waiting nets.

Bruce's charming wife, Joy, who had dedicated her life to furthering Bruce's career, listened in rapt silence as we outlined our plans for a joint expedition to Rangiroa Atoll the following year. Nearly every great man in history has had the guiding influence of a devoted woman, perhaps in the background, but always there to counsel and to help. Joy is such a woman, destined to remain unknown to all but a fortunate few.

Bruce planned to return to French Polynesia during the following "dry season" months, to evaluate the sonic approach to shark repellents. The expedition was planned to be small and compact, with about six members, including Joy. We tentatively set the month of August 1969 for our venture. At the end of the seminar I reluctantly took my leave and returned to Rangiroa, filled with hope for the future. At last it appeared I had overcome my problems and was on the wide and straight path to success.

I wanted to see what would happen if I continued to transmit distress stimulus for extended periods. Already I could move packs of sharks, even when in the frenzied state, for distances of up to several hundred feet. I simply had to alter the location of the attractive signals. First I transmitted distress stimulus, calling in the sharks to one area. Once they became excited and frenzied, I would immediately discontinue the signals and would begin transmitting the sounds in another locality, anything from 50 feet to several hundred feet away. I found that the sharks immediately responded and moved en masse to the new transmission area. But what would happen if I continued the signals for an unlimited period? Would the sharks become conditioned and cease to respond to the attractive signals? This was a question that I had to find the answer to.

I carefully concealed my transducer in a small coral cavern beneath a large overhanging coral bombie. This was to ensure that the unit was inaccessible to the attracted sharks, for I had to safeguard the transducers from any possibility of damage. Of all my equipment, only these vital units had given a faultless performance.

In a matter of a few seconds a number of sharks had responded to the sounds and were excitedly darting around the coral that concealed the transducer. The attractive signals continued, and more sharks arrived to join those already milling about far below me. They were becoming agitated as their short, violent manoeuvres showed—and then, without warning, one of the sharks charged the small opening under the coral. The entrance to the little cavern was so narrow that the shark became tightly wedged in it and was unable to move further. More sharks immediately followed suit, and charged at the signal source with uncontrolled fury. It was as though the animals had become consumed by rage and were no longer able to control their movements. Their efforts jammed them tightly in the remaining opening. Other sharks now began to batter themselves to death on the surrounding corals, and I could hear the sickening crunch and thuds as they rammed their heads into the unyielding limestone. Sharks then attacked and savaged those jammed in the cave entrance, tearing great hunks of flesh from their bodies. Those lying insensible on the lagoon floor were also mauled. For the first time in my long association with sharks I felt emotionally disturbed. The scene disgusted me, and I felt quite ill. I stopped the signals, for I had seen enough. Later I counted nine sharks packed into an opening so small that I had been forced to wriggle in backwards to set up the transducer. These sharks were jammed in so tightly that I had to attach heavy rope to their protruding tails, and pull them out one by one with the aid of the outboard-powered boat.

I conducted a number of such experiments and each time I was rewarded with the same results. Sharks battering themselves to death in a sickening suicide frenzy, all in the effort to reach the source of the attractive sound vibrations. As Robert later remarked in disgust, "At least you have found a sure way of getting rid of the bludgers: let them bash their own brains out."

It was time to go. Mama was weeping quietly as Robbie and I boarded the DC-4 for the flight back to Papeete. We could barely see above the layers of shells that encircled our necks. Robert's Tahitian girl-friends waved enthusiastically as we peered through the aircraft windows at the crowd gathered to farewell us. All our Tahitian friends had come: Jumbo, the Little Bloke, Theodore, Jules, Papa and Mama and the boys, and even Jean Tehahe, the post master at Avatoru, whom Robert had nicknamed "Stirling Moss" because of the breakneck speed at which he drove the bus to the airport to meet each flight and collect the mail. And then we were alone in the sky, each with his own thoughts and memories, some pleasant, some sad, some bitter. Robert was eager to return to Australia and home; I was already planning my next programme and my return to French Polynesia.

It was six in the evening when Marcus and I arrived home at East Lindfield after a frantic day of last-minute arrangements, for it was the evening of my departure to Tahiti for the 1969 research season. My flight was scheduled to depart from the Sydney airport at

8 p.m., and I hadn't even packed, let alone showered, shaved and dressed. The drive to the airport would take at least 30 to 40 minutes, and this depended on the traffic being light.

"I'll never make it, Bol," I groaned to my brother.

"Ah yes, you will, Jock," he replied as he frantically flung clothes and equipment together in my two suitcases. "Give them a ring and tell 'em you'll be late."

I sprang into action and telephoned the chief traffic control officer of Qantas at the airport. Briefly I informed him who I was and added that I would be unable to make the airport before about 7.45 p.m.

"But all passengers must be cleared by Immigration before that time and already aboard the flight," came the reply.

"Well," I said, grabbing the bull by the horns, "I know the managing director of Qantas, Captain Ritchie personally." This was really not a lie for I had met Captain Ritchie after asking Qantas for assistance in my research undertaking. "Shall I call him and see what he can do?"

"No, that won't be necessary," came the reply. "Just get here as quickly as possible, and remember I cannot hold the flight after 8 p.m."

It was 7.55 p.m. when, accompanied by Marcus, I presented myself at the Qantas counter in a breathless state. My baggage was quickly seized and I was hurried to the embarkation gate where the Immigration officer took my already completed departure card, and stamped my passport. I was ushered out into the darkness to the waiting aircraft and ran up the stairs. As I entered, the door was swung shut behind me. The hostess who showed me to my seat remarked that she had never seen that happen before, to which I growled in reply, "All part of the Qantas service." As the aircraft taxied away and I settled into my seat I heard someone sarcastically remark, "Those damn V.I.P's can do what they like." When I landed at Papeete airport some hours later, there waiting on the tarmac were Lieut.-Colonel Garnier and Andy Babst, complete with an official car on which fluttered two miniature French flags. Even the crew and passengers were impressed as I stepped off the plane to be greeted with colourful flower leis and warm embraces.

It was late June of 1969, and I had returned as the co-director of the joint French-American World Life Expedition to Rangiroa Atoll. This had developed into an impressive affair since its modest start almost a year before when Bruce Halstead and I had planned the small research undertaking. There were now twenty American scientists and assistants, a photographic team from the Brooks Institute in California to record the entire research programme on colour motion film, and the Tahitian staff members who were to assist. The expedition included Dr Don Nelson and his assistant, Richard Johnson, who were working with underwater sound for the Office of Naval Research in Washington. Don's programme was unfortunately distinct from mine, in that his research centred around attracting sharks with pulsed signal tones, whereas I was employing naturally recorded distress stimulus, refined and modified in the laboratory. And Don wasn't involved with the repellent aspects of sound, the most important part of my programme.

Bruce had decided that my electronic equipment would not be needed, since Don Nelson was fully equipped; and this unlucky decision was seriously to restrict the research undertaking. Dr Nelson's gear, although suitable and adequate for his programme, could not be adapted to meet the requirements and techniques of my work; and so I was again brought to a virtual standstill before I started. I was to spend another frustrating and unrewarding research season in French Polynesia. This I found heartbreaking, for I was already well behind with my programme, and I had looked forward to the opportunity of being able to work in close co-operation with Don. We were both bitterly disappointed that this chance was denied to us.

It was July when we arrived back at Rangiroa, I to the fond greeting of my many Tahitian friends, and the others to a new experience and the making of new friendships. We settled into two rented houses at Avatoru which Dr Bagnis had arranged for us. These were pleasant and cool and suitable to our needs. Mama lost little time in inviting the entire expedition over for dinner, and for the occasion "Pooer" the pig met an untimely end. "Where is Robert?" demanded Mama in her broken English. I explained that Rob was well and sent his fondest wishes, but he had to remain in Australia to finish his schooling. Mama and Papa were greatly disappointed but understood.

The Brooks Institute boys, Ernie Brooks, Jr, Mal Wolfe, and Gene Cornelius, had constructed a huge shark cage and shipped this to Rangiroa. From this they intended to film my shark research in comfort and safety. Disaster almost struck when the cage was being taken out to its resting-place in the maelstrom area. It was raised and lowered through the water by means of a floatation bag. But a sudden surge in the current seized the slowly sinking cage and carried it towards the entrance pass at an alarming speed. Quickly the divers inflated the bag and the cage bobbed to the surface, there to be taken in tow by the waiting boat. The current proved too much for the outboard-powered boat, and soon all were being swept back into the pass and in danger of being carried out to sea. Some passing Tahitians in a larger boat came to our assistance, and the runaway cage was soon on its way back to the maelstrom.

Finally, after considerable trouble, the Brooks boys positioned their cage firmly on the lagoon floor in 55 feet of water. Massive chains anchored it to its supporting stand, and these were sufficient to prevent even the strongest current or surge from endangering its stability. The cage was a huge affair that could comfortably accommodate six divers, and was designed to withstand the onslaughts of the most bad-tempered of sharks. But at first it frightened the sharks, and they would not come near to this strange apparition that towered above the corals and white sand plains. It took some days before they became conditioned and ceased to be afraid; then they completely ignored the cage and would even swim beneath its supporting legs.

One day while Mal and Gene were comfortably settled in their cage to do some filming, a large barracuda, six feet or more in length, swam casually through the narrow bars and into the cage. It continued on through to the other side and emerged to swim leisurely on its way. There was some commotion in the cage, and Mal and Gene shot to the surface to make hurried arrangements for the placing of finer wire mesh around their underwater retreat.

But there were no Grey Sharks. The hundreds upon hundreds that had inhabited the lagoon were gone. Not even the maelstrom could offer a single Grey and only a few White-tips remained.

The mystery was soon solved by Jumbo and Theodore, who explained that during July the sharks always went away. No one knew why, or where the sharks migrated to; but it was always the same each year, and during August thousands would flock back into the lagoon, to remain for another year. Then I remembered that during July of the previous year I had caught almost no sharks. Because of my equipment failures and strong trade winds I had not dived in the maelstrom during the entire month, and so I had not missed the sharks. Where they migrate to is a mystery that remains to be solved, for the same thing happens at other lagoons in the Tuamotus. Somewhere, perhaps close at hand, will one day be found what may be the greatest assembly of sharks witnessed by man, for this yearly migratory movement must involve hundreds of thousands of sharks.

The expedition resulted in much worthwhile research, and despite my lack of involvement with the sharks I was kept fully occupied and had little spare time. The Brooks boys were always present, with cameras grinding both on the surface and under water, and I was soon dubbed "Captain Kangaroo" by Mal and Gene. Since they required a considerable footage of sharks in action, we spent much time searching the lagoon for the elusive Greys. The lack of sharks greatly hampered Dr Nelson's research with underwater sound transmission. And Dr Glen Egstrom, from the University of California, who had intended to investigate and record the divers' reactions and behaviour in a shark infested environment, also had his programme frustrated.

Bruce had chartered a 40-foot launch for the month's expedition, and this enabled us to undertake a detailed survey of the lagoon and of the several small islands in the centre of it. At one such island we encountered a large school of manta rays, and were able to spend an enjoyable thirty minutes swimming with these massive but gentle creatures. We visited the neighbouring atoll of Tikehau, but this had also been deserted by the sharks. During the last few days of July, and while Andy Babst was visiting Rangiroa, I saw the first few Grey Sharks moving back into the waters of the lagoon. But the expedition had completed its alloted time of one month, and we reluctantly packed up and left the atoll.

I remained in Tahiti with Andy until September, when the Brooks boys were scheduled to return. Mal and Gene wished to film some of the Grey Sharks, and I had agreed to accompany them back to the atoll for several weeks. I was greatly relieved on our first dive out in the maelstrom to see many sharks lazing about on the lagoon floor. On diving down I was soon surrounded by the familiar forms, milling aimlessly in and out of the corals. Papa quickly put an end to the tranquillity of the scene when he speared a large cod: there was a flurry of activity and a minor skirmish as the struggling fish was seized and devoured by a hungry Grey. "Yooooooooo Hooooooooo ma'o back", came Papa's delighted cry.

During my stay in Tahiti plans were made for a continuation of my research programme. After discussions with Dr Saugrain it was decided that the work would be spread over the 1970 and 1971 research seasons. Although Colonel Garnier was scheduled to return to the south of France, there to take command of a paratroopers' regiment, I was assured of continued assistance by his replacement, Commandant André. During an official luncheon with the new Governor, His Excellency Monsieur Pierre Angeli, I was given the opportunity of explaining and outlining the sonic approach to shark repellents. Both the Governor and Madame Angeli were greatly interested in the outcome of the programme and since both spoke excellent English, I was questioned at some length.

To obtain the additional financial support I needed for my work I had made application to the Australian Research Grants Committee during 1969.

I had been granted an affiliation with the School of Biological Sciences of the University of Sydney, by the head of the School, Professor L. C. Birch, after an investigation and evaluation of my shark research by Dr Gordon Grigg of the Zoology Department. This enabled me to make application to the Commonwealth Government for assistance. I urgently needed money to enable the project to be completely reorganized, and my application was supported by Dr Halstead and Dr Perry Gilbert.

I intended to purchase a high-speed launch and fully equip this as a floating laboratory. To make possible the research I planned on the dangerous White Shark and other pelagic species I intended to use underwater closed-circuit television to monitor the experiments. I would not have to enter the water, but could control all future research into the sonic approach from the comfort and, more important, the safety of the laboratory, simply by watching the television screen. Important data could be recorded and stored for future reference on videotape. The launch, being fully self-contained with an ocean-going laboratory, would greatly reduce the overall costs involved in keeping the programme operative. On the completion of research in Australian waters during the summer months, it would simply be loaded onto a cargo steamer and shipped to Polynesia, or to a selected overseas research location, where it would be ready for immediate use. Applications were also lodged with the Premiers of the Victorian, New South Wales and Queensland State Governments for additional assistance. All were engaged in shark meshing programmes to protect their major bathing beaches, and it was pointed out that the successful application of the sonic approach would greatly reduce their long-term expenditure on shark protection, as well as ensure that the method employed was completely foolproof. But my coming involvement with the Crown of Thorns starfish was to wreck any chance I had of getting any help, financial or otherwise, from the Australian political machine.

On returning to Australia in October 1969 I made arrangements to go to Magnetic Island and the Great Barrier Reef. Bruce Halstead had asked me to form a small expedition to examine the reef and the threat posed by the Crown of Thorns. I was to spend only the summer months on the reef, and was to return to Tahiti in the following April for the 1970 season.

Before leaving Sydney I visited the scene of Ken's tragic attack. It was a cold, windy day, and I found the waters dirty and polluted. The clean yellow sand I remembered was now discoloured and littered with broken tree branches and trash. It was a depressing visit, for I felt so far from achieving my goal: of making Ken's death stand for something, making it serve some purpose. "Perhaps", I thought as I stood silently on the wet sand, "my next visit to French Polynesia will put me well on the road to success." I still had my hope and determination to succeed.

Since I was to conduct sonic experimental work with the starfish, I decided that I could further my shark project at the same time. Dr W. H. Dawbin, of the Zoology Department of the

Sydney University, who lived close to my home in East Lindfield, had recently returned from New Guinea where he had done some interesting research with dolphins. Dr Dawbin was investigating the reactions of dolphins to certain sound frequencies, knowing that some New Guinea tribes used sound to round-up and capture the animals.

The natives would head out into open deep water in their canoes and hunt for a school of dolphins. When it was found, the school would be driven towards the shore by sound vibrations. Knocking stones together under water, the natives were able to round-up the dolphins, and once in shallow water the sounds were intensified. As soon as waist-deep water was reached, the stone-knocking increased until a crescendo of noise echoed through the water. The resulting frequencies became so unbearable to the trapped dolphins that they attempted to drive their heads into the mud and coral of the sea floor. They were quickly caught and slaughtered by the encircling natives. Dr Dawbin had reliable reports that the catch often exceeded many hundreds of the unfortunate animals, entire schools being killed at the one time.

Of extreme interest to me was the fact that during the entire procedure the natives were never bothered by sharks. This I found difficult to understand, for the region was frequented by such dangerous species as the Tiger and Whaler Sharks, and the confusion and "distress stimulus" echoing outwards through the water while the dolphins were being slaughtered should have "called-in" every shark in the vicinity. In addition, on witnessing the colour motion film Dr Dawbin was kind enough to screen for my benefit, I saw that the surrounding water was soon red with blood as dozens of these lovely creatures were killed. It was a depressing sight, and I was informed that efforts were being made by the authorities in New Guinea to convince the natives that the practice should stop. This will be difficult, since the tribes have been slaughtering dolphins by this method for as long as the villagers can remember.

Why didn't sharks respond to the attractive sound vibrations from the death struggles of the dolphins? Or why didn't they respond to the attractive olfactory stimulus provided by the large quantities of blood spilling into the surrounding waters? To perhaps provide an answer to these questions, Dr Dawbin gave me a short tape recording of the underwater noises made during the natives' stone-knocking activities. I intended to experiment with this tape while on the Great Barrier Reef, and determine if the sounds were capable of repelling sharks from the vicinity of "distress stimulus", for this appeared to be the logical answer.

Dr Dawbin is a world authority on the study of whales, and during a discussion of his recent research I learnt that some species of whale were capable of transmitting sounds under water over a radius of several hundred miles. This I found astounding, for my efforts had been restricted to a mile or so at their best.

I was able to achieve little worthwhile research on my arrival in North Queensland. When I entered into the starfish controversy I became the target of political bias as members of parliament fought to preserve their "image" regardless of the cost to the nation. I soon became bogged down with the Crown of Thorns problem, and I still am. The innocent act of engaging in starfish research has involved me in one of the most bitter struggles of my career. I became caught in the warring factions of the academic world, as one side cried down the alarm and concern expressed by the other. So disgusted did I become with the political interference of the Queensland Government that at one stage I was considering abandoning marine research altogether.

Twice because of my involvement with the Crown of Thorns problem I have been forced to cancel my return to French Polynesia and the continuation of my shark research. Three long years have dragged by, and during this time my shark programme has been restricted to the tagging of sharks and the capture of specimens for bioligical examination purposes. The starfish consume most of my time and energy. But I have not been alone in my struggles, for I have had the support and guidance of such senior scientists and friends as Dr Robert Endean, Isobel Bennett, Dr Gordon Grigg, Dr Richard Chesher, Dr Perry Gilbert, and Dr Bruce Halstead and his wonderful wife Joy, as well as their daughter, Linda, with her husband, Bob.

The greater the obstacles that present themselves, the more determined I am becoming to continue my shark research programme. Once my involvement with the Crown of Thorns starfish has run its course I shall return to the sharks, and I shall feel safer surrounded by these primitive animals than dealing with politicians.

During the recent cyclone "Althea" that devastated much of Townsville and Magnetic Island, where I am still based, I suffered a further serious set-back. Much of my electronic equipment and scientific records was lost in the fury of the cyclone, which sent winds of unbelievable violence to lash the island. Some have estimated that gusts at the peak of the blow were in the vicinity of 200 miles per hour, and on viewing the shocking damage to Magnetic Island this does not appear to be an exaggeration. It is amazing how one's values change in times of extreme stress. At the start of "Althea" my only concern was to ensure the safety of my equipment and records. The building that served as my house and laboratory was soundly constructed, and I watched the surrounding homes being unroofed and demolished before my eyes as the winds increased in strength. Some buildings when unroofed collapsed like wet cardboard, losing all shape and identity. Others staggered under the onslaught of the screeching wind to disintegrate piece by piece. As my home started to tremble under the increasing pressure I ceased to be concerned about the welfare of my possessions. When the roof was torn off in one terrifying second I forgot everything and retreated to the safety offered beneath the bed. Here, lying in several inches of water, and surrounded by my sodden records, I peered out at the nightmare storm, wondering if I would survive.

Much of value was lost for ever. But I was later able to salvage a good deal of my irreplaceable records and some of my electronic equipment. Many on the island lost all they possessed, and were without home or money. On driving around when the winds had eased I found that "Althea" had reaped a shocking toll. The valley where Picnic Bay had once been looked as though the area had been blasted by an atomic bomb, for the destruction was unbelievable; few homes were left standing and none remained untouched. The naked trees, those remaining upright, gave the entire bay the appearance of a graveyard, leafless branches pointing their fingers accusingly towards the heavens. It was so desolate and depressing a scene that my problems and loss became insignificant: here I was surrounded by shattered hopes and dreams, by human misery and anguish.

I am planning for the day when I'll be able to continue my research. For I know that with the sonic approach to shark repellents I hold the key, the key to open a door that has been closed to man so long.

Index

131

Theo Brown was born in Melbourne. During his pioneering work on the sonic approach to shark repellents, he has become an internationally known marine scientist. His ongoing shark program, interrupted in 1969 to study the crown of thorns star-fish problem on the Great Barrier Reef, has now been resumed on Rangiroa in French Polynesia. Mr. Brown is the author (with Keith Willey) of Crown of Thorns: The Death of the Great Barrier Reef?, published in 1972.

Theo Brown is a Marine Research Associate of the World Life Research Institute (a United States Government subsidized or-ganization) of Colton, California and of the Medical Oceanog-raphic Branch of the Louis Malarde Institute of Medical Research of French Polynesia. He was recently appointed as a Consultant to the South Pacific Commission on Pollution of the Marine Environment. He works in close association with the Department of Fisheries of French Polynesia; with Dr. Perry W. Gilbert of the Mote Marine Laboratory, Florida; with the Shark Research Panel of the American Institute of Biological Sciences; and with the Office of Naval Research, United States Navy, Washington — as well as with Australian and other overseas scientific research institutions and universities.